G000041746

Acclaim for *Antido*

"*Antidote to Overwhelm* is a totally accessible and practical invitation to live a fuller life.

It is rare for someone to have a stable awareness of the present moment; much more so to be able to articulate that experience in writing. Dr. Cheryl Kasdorf is one of those people."

Greg Hopkinson, author & Film Producer,
A Mindful Choice

"It seems like meditation is the new black, and everyone from athletes, performers, executives and entrepreneurs are attributing their success to being more in the present moment. This book, written by meditation teacher Dr. Cheryl Kasdorf, shows us why this is the case, and what is possible for all of us when start to live in the Now.

Critical reading for anyone dealing with overwhelm, doubt and confusion."

Peter Cook, author & CEO of Thought Leaders Global

"I teach 'presence' because it's a path to spiritual realization and to a rich, joyful, and fulfilling life.

Antidote to Overwhelm is a great instruction to deepen your own presence and significantly reduce the stress in your life."

Rachael Jayne Groover,
author of *Powerful and Feminine*

"*Antidote to Overwhelm* provides a simple, clear description of what creates stress in our lives, and how to let that stress go. It is direct, simple and often humorous.

The book also provides clear instruction and exercises on how to actually experience what it means to be truly present. *Antidote to Overwhelm* is a wonderful resource for anyone who wants to be the best version of themselves they can be."

Narain Ishaya, author of *Chit Happens, A Guide to Discovering Divinity*

We are so lucky to finally be able to drink from Dr. Cheryl's decades of experience and focused research in one proven "Antidote to Overwhelm."

Loto Vázquez, author & Founder of The Happiness Social Network

"Dr. Cheryl Kasdorf has masterfully described how to bring the aliveness of NOW back into our lives. We are taken out of the realm of theory and invited to experientially live in this moment. This is the invaluable uniqueness of the book.

Far beyond being inspirational, which it is, it's a practical solution to life's problems. What we really want is the Antidote!"

Paramananda Ishaya, author of *A Path of Joy*

Contents

Introduction   xiii

I. What is "resting in this present moment?"   1

The rest of your life?   3

1.1 Peak Experiences   5

1.2 Effortlessness   9

1.3 What interferes with peace   13

1.4 Now, not past or future   19

1.5 Rest, productivity & getting things done   21

1.6 Body cycles / Earth cycles   25

1.7 Rest is the prime state of
getting things done   29

1.8 A game to make resting Now simple   39

1.9 More play with resting Now   47

1.10 Resting is a feat, let's compete!   51

1.11 Resting in a body   55

1.12 Bad day/good day   61

1.13 Judgment, emotions, action and rest   69

    No rest with judgment   71

    Feelings and judgment   73

    All experiences   75

1.14 What removes us from resting   79

    Rest with emotions   80

    Resting in Challenges   82

1.15 Resting, Alertness, Thoughts   89

1.16 Gentleness and Stillness
     and Compassion   99

1.17 Our natural state vs. suffering   103

1.18 The highest form of prayer   111

II. The world we create resting in
this eternal present   119

2.1 The Golden Universe   121

"Being present is not about paying attention to this moment, and this moment, and this moment.

Becoming aware of the infinite presence that underlies this reality, resting in an eternal moment, being completely alive for the rest of your life; that's living.

That is truly living. That is what you are here for."

— M. Krishnananda Ishaya

Peak Experiences

Wasn't it beautiful when you have, starkly and simply, experienced a most wonderful moment in your life? Wasn't it lovely? I know you have, even if you do not remember it right now.

Maybe it was at the crest of a hill, on a trail during a hike, overlooking a scene that took your breath away. Or looking into the innocent and pure face of a baby and catching the look in her eyes. Or it might have been in the midst of a game, when you were in the zone and made the perfect play, seemingly as if in slow motion.

Beauty and perfection were overwhelmingly present and you felt totally all right with the world. Nothing could make that moment any better. And nothing could take anything away from the wonder and beauty and stillness of that moment.

All this was because all the cares of your day-to-day life in the world dropped away. You were not worrying about the meeting with your boss or anticipating what would happen when you could not fulfill an obligation. You were not regretting your response to your spouse hours ago.

The past and future dropped away, and you were left with being right here, right now, in wonder and awe and love of life happening in this moment.

Whether it was connecting with the innocence of a baby, making the shot in the game, or being swept away by the beauty of nature, you were totally engrossed in that experience and nothing else mattered. Nothing else existed at that point, because you had a single-focused attention on what was happening right in front of you.

The magic of the experience could have lingered, even if the height of the experience faded away. You remember this experience and it sticks with you long after it has gone. It sticks as a peak moment in your life.

We remember those peak moments because they are so fulfilling, and they make us feel right with the world. They remind us that we can love life. They may come back to us when we are in the midst of a tough time, because they give us the sense that life doesn't have to be hard. We may think that life would be so much better if we could see beauty all around and all the angst of the problems of life would just drop away.

It can be.

That which you experienced for just moments can be a constant experience. That's exactly what it means to rest in this present moment. When you do, this present moment seems to last forever.

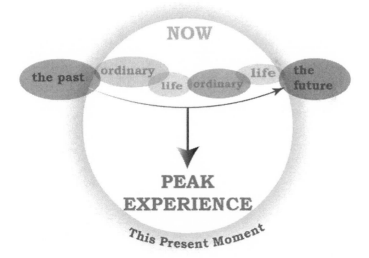

All it takes is the willingness to drop all the ways that you were before, which actually weren't working for you, even if you thought they were. All it takes is the willingness to settle into the awareness of Now, where life takes care of itself.

What you need is presented to you now. You see it because you are alert to it and not distracted by thoughts of the past or future. There is no effort while resting in this present moment. Life seems to take care of itself!

You will want to jump for joy and dance and shout. Everyone will hear you shouting and singing but you don't care as you rest in this present moment.

You feel so good, you feel so right in yourself. You feel so at home that you want to rest here forever. This is the place of ease and flow.

1.2

Effortlessness

The ego is not a thing but a subtle effort, and you cannot use effort to get rid of effort — you end up with two efforts instead of one. The ego itself is a perfect manifestation of the Divine, and it is best handled by resting in Freedom, not by trying to get rid of ego, which simply increases the effort of the ego itself.

— Ken Wilber, *The Simple Feeling of Being*

When we are resting in this present moment, everything seems easy and flowing because there is no effort. Effort is a thing of the past. Effort is too much bother to ever consider. Effort is a joke when life is lived in this way. When effort is for the most part a thing of the past, it can be a marker now, a litmus test to determine when we have dropped out of the awareness of the present.

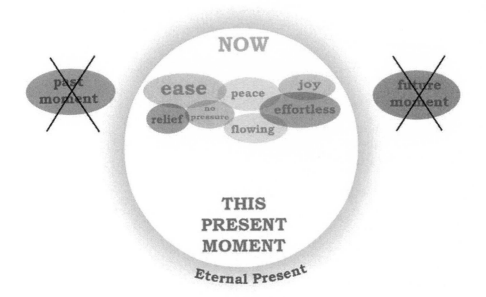

Let me tell you about a time when I was entrenched in effort. Are you surprised? I was known for being a hard worker, and I made an effort to work hard.

Yes, there were times when I put in lots of effort in order to do things and get things. And you know what? The more effort I put in, it seems, the less I got out. Being a hard worker satisfied the need to achieve what I thought I needed to achieve.

I did not want to be seen as lazy. If I did not do well or achieve what I wanted to, I did not want it to be because I did not work hard for it. I did not want to be at fault for not working hard enough.

The only joy I got was at the end of the work, looking back at it and knowing I had worked hard and achieved something. But while doing the hard work, I was not enjoying it so much. I delayed the enjoyment for the end.

When it was finished, or if it was ever finished, I could enjoy it. But I did not enjoy it so much because at the end, the feeling was fleeting as another project came up and I applied myself to it. And sometimes the project was never done, so I never even got the satisfaction of completion.

The more effort I put into doing something or achieving something, the less I enjoyed it – both getting it and having it. Once I had the fruits of my hard effort, I did not enjoy it much. It was as if I simply returned to a baseline of having something, then looking ahead to achieving something more.

The more effort I put in, the more squeezed my life felt. The pressure was there to achieve even more in the future. That is no way to live! That is life without joy.

You see, I had made achievement and efficiency my goal in life. It happened without thinking about it, without considering what I was doing.

Later, when asked what I wanted most in my life, my immediate answer was "peace."

Was it peace because that is what would relieve me from the pressure of achieving efficiently? I just knew that I had experienced the relief of not having to do and not having to achieve and that was peace.

Since then, I have discovered a depth and strength in peace that I did not imagine possible.

1.3

What interferes with peace

In order to rest peacefully, it appeared to me that I had to find and remove what was interfering with my peace.

Of course, this is an endless game, because when you look for something, you will find it. Then as you look for something else, you will find that too. There will be no end to finding what might be interfering with peace.

I had a tendency to play a game about finding what was interfering with my peace. It is a simple game. I'll bet you have played this game too.

The game goes like this: If I figure out what I did wrong in the past, I should be able to figure out how I can do it better in the future. The purpose of figuring out how to do it better next time is to avoid the pain and frustration of doing it wrong.

I went over and over and over in my mind, re-hashing a situation in which I was not aware what I had done, but it had "bad" consequences. The consequences were that someone was criticizing me, telling me that I did not communicate well, and because of how I reacted, I hurt her.

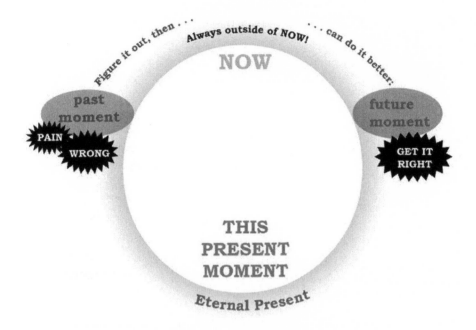

Can you bring to mind a similar situation that happened to you? It may have been just yesterday or a long time ago; it doesn't matter. It may still be hanging around and bothering you.

I first went into blaming her and making myself right. That bought me a few moments of ease for myself, but anger about her.

When I realized what I was doing, I saw that blaming would not help me figure out how to do it better next time. Therefore, I stopped blaming and tried to figure out what had happened so I would have a baseline understanding.

Then I felt confused, and had no idea what had happened — so of course, I was absolved of any responsibility and action. How could I figure out how to do it better if I had no idea what was happening? I was safe for the moment.

Again, that made me feel better temporarily, but it did not tell me how to do it better next time.

Then I tried to figure out her communication style, her mode of operating in the world. That way I could see how I could respond in a way that she would understand through her communication style.

That was a lot of work, with a lot of speculation! How could I know for sure that the next time something like this happened, I would remember the right way to respond — that is, in a way that would make her happy? There was no assurance. It was exhausting.

The best that my mind could figure out was to let her communicate in her way and always respond "thank you" to whatever she said. That would diffuse the situation, and perhaps let her know she was being heard.

However, that would not stop my split-second reaction before a "thank you" could come out. What if I said something besides "thank you" first?

I kept plugging away at it, on and on, trying to figure out this situation. If something like this happened in the future, what could I do in that moment to make it come out right?

What changed the game for me, and what I recommend for you, is to not spend a single moment more on it.

Don't spend any more time on that situation, analyzing what went wrong and seeing how you could change to do it better next time. If apologies are in order, then make them, but you will never fix that original situation.

To attempt to fix a past situation is coming from a perspective of life as broken, so you can fix it. I know now that there is no way for it to never happen again. I don't have control over that.

In fact, it is not the situation that went "badly" that is the issue. The issue is going back and trying to figure it out how to do it better in the future. That was taking me out of resting in THIS moment.

I know it is useless to want to change the past. It is useless to dwell on the past and attempt to re-do it. I have tried it! If you have ever tried it, you know too that the situation and time are gone. The energy is gone.

When I hung on to the situation, wanting to re-do it, THAT was painful for me.

That game was causing me pain, and now I am done with pain. I hope you are done with pain too. There is none of this kind of pain resting in this present moment.

Let's look at this differently and play a different game.

Since the situation is in the past, let's leave it in the past. Since we can only go forward from now, then let's leave it.

Also, let's not even try to do it better in the future. The future is not here. How do we know what will be presented in the future? Most likely it will not be the same, and the response will be inappropriate. The future will take care of itself.

Let's simply rest now in this present moment.

Present-moment awareness has taken care of trying to do it better. All by itself.

Resting now, is there any better and any worse?

My experience is that there is only what is being presented, and that fills my whole experience. There is nothing else to compare it to. Therefore, there is no better and worse.

There is only the fullness and beauty of now.

1.4

Now, not past or future

The future is unknown.

There is only Now.

Let's not waste our Now looking to the past or looking to the future. This Now is incredibly full; let's not deflate that fullness by going backwards to the past or forward to the future.

When we know that Now is the only place we want to be, then let's be here. Now. Be here. No straying.

It took so much energy to try to figure out what happened in the past, didn't it? And could you figure it out?

The effort of trying to figure out the past is wasted energy. You'll see that as you stop doing it. You'll feel how much energy is liberated by not going back to the past to figure it out. You'll feel so much energy just staying here Now.

One day I decided that I'd had enough of my cold that was hanging on. I knew that it was helping me to release old stuff, and that was fine with me. However, resting in the now releases old stuff as well.

Resting now has no past to it, so what was in the past has no relevance.

I said to myself, why not rest deeply in now, and forget about the middleman of the snot in my nose? Yeah, why not?

As I rested deeply, the deep rest transformed into no longer being aware that I was aware. Then a short time later (it seemed), I was able to be alert and aware, and to breathe better through my nose. There was less snot. The headache was gone.

Wow – how was that for less effort?

That is the power of resting in this present moment.

1.5

Rest, productivity & getting things done

This is the beginning of the rest of your life. Yes, the REST of your life.

There is an idea that rest has to do with being nonproductive. Yes, in the moments we are resting, we are not obviously being productive. Nothing is being produced when we rest.

However, productivity is only meaningful over the long run. When we do not rest, it is not possible to be productive in the long run. Rest is the hidden element of productivity. It is an essential element in order to truly be productive.

Have you ever pushed late into the night to get something done? I have. The more tired I was, the longer it took. How's that for low productivity?

On the other hand, it could have been more productive to sleep and rest, then work on it the next day.

Many times I have done that, and it has worked out beautifully. I didn't worry about it; I simply went to bed and set the alarm a little early. Then I was fresh to finish my project. It certainly was more enjoyable that way.

Spending time sleeping makes my time more productive, because I get it done faster when I am rested. In addition, when resting, I am open to messages from my unconscious mind. I can let down the guard of the conscious mind and let the solution or inspiration come to me.

Using rest this way is highly underrated. But this use of rest is the essential hidden element of productivity.

In addition, productivity has been elevated to false heights. What good is productivity as the goal of life?

1.7

Rest is the prime state of getting things done

Beyond rest being the other side of activity, beyond rest being a half of a polarity, rest is an absolute state. In fact, rest is the prime state of getting things done.

How can that be? What I am talking about is not the activity-rest cycle. What I am talking about is when we let activity come from the state of rest, that state of rest can be maintained in activity.

When we let activity come from resting in this present moment, we can be active while resting here, now. It sounds like a contradiction, so I will explain further.

Resting in this present moment is our natural state, and it has everything we need in it. Resting here is like seeing with an unblinking eye.

This present moment sees all, resting in its seeing. It does not miss anything in its seeing, because it is unblinking.

All is contained in the seeing while resting. It contains all in potential.

The unblinking eye of this present moment is seeing the eternal Now. It is omniscient and omnipresent because it goes beyond time to rest as the eternal Now. All is contained in the eternal Now, and all is seen by the unblinking eye.

Now is not one moment as now, then the next moment as now, then the next, then the next. The Now of this eternal present is not a string of nows experienced individually, sequentially in time. This eternal Now is beyond time and space. Now as this Eternal Present contains all, and all rests in it.

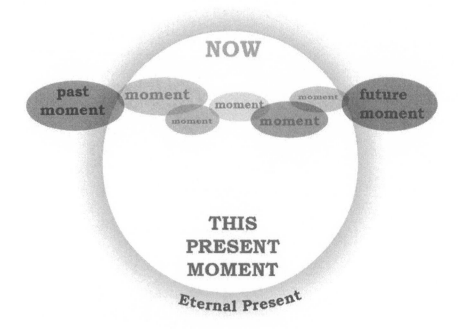

Therefore, this eternal present of the unblinking eye contains the possibility of creation. In creating something,

In experiencing that there is nothing to do, how can we possibly get things done?

While resting Now, I am totally content to just be here. It feels natural to be just here. There is such a vibrant aliveness; I am engaging all of life.

Just being here, how can I get things done?

There is no impulse to be anywhere else but immersed in this present moment. Therefore, there is no movement out of this experience of Now. There is no other experience but the engagement of all of life. In engaging life, I am playing with all that is.

How is playing with all that is getting things done?

All is contained in this now. In being alive in this now, resting here, I see life happening. I see what could be termed "my life" happening.

All that happens, happens of itself. That means there is no effort for anything to happen, and I am involved in it happening. It is a thrill to be involved in the happening of life.

While life is happening as I am resting deeply in Now, things are getting done. In fact, the wisdom of Now gets things done in a better way than I could imagine them happening.

You mean, I don't have to get things done, and they get done?

Yes. Since Now contains all, resting in Now is engaging what every part of now wants to happen. There is a seamless coordination of happening, because every part is engaged. The best happens for each and every part of all while resting deeply in Now, this present moment.

This is how I experience resting in this present moment, in Now, as being the prime state of getting things done. They get done because they happen of themselves. I am engaged in this happening in a restful, complete way. It is supremely enjoyable.

You have probably felt that at some time in your life. Some time when life sparkled and everything seemed like a miracle. When the enjoyment of life was front and center, and there was no effort at all.

At that time, effortlessness was not a goal, but life was happening effortlessly. What you knew you had to do got done almost as if you were watching someone else do it.

In addition, there was even more done which you had no idea wanted to be done.

That is the state of resting in now and seeing things happen. That is the absolute activity-generating power of resting.

Instead of being lazy, indolent, not caring to do work, this kind of resting is the key to effortlessness. It is the key to ease and joy. It is the key to a life well lived.

As resting in Now is our natural state, it is effortless. Life feels really alive and vibrant. The feeling is so fulfilling that we know that is why we were put on Earth. We know that life must be lived like this.

Sometimes when I notice I am doing with effort, I remember that state of resting, and want to get back to it. However, I then put effort into getting back there. That is the biggest trap!

By putting effort into resting, I have already defeated my purpose. I have tricked myself into thinking that even if just for a moment, I apply anything other than effortlessness and ease to resting, I will be able to return to it.

Not so! Resting is the ultimate in effortlessness, and putting any effort into resting is, by definition, not resting. Resting is simply easing back and letting go. It is letting action happen through me. It is simple.

In that case, how do I return to resting when I catch myself putting out effort?

By simply resting. It is our natural state. There is no trick to it.

I simply let go and rest softly in Now, only Now, to the ease of just Now. I gently rest in this present moment.

Nothing else exists. Only what is here Now, in this present moment, exists. None of the backlog of the past can touch the rest of this present moment. None of the anticipation of the future applies to this present moment. Only the gentle, restful, vibrant, alert experience of this present moment is here.

You see how simple it is?

By remembering only Now, resting happens. By resting in Now, resting happens without effort. By resting in now, things happen without effort.

It sounds like a trick, but it isn't. It's just that simple if you allow it to be.

Stop for a moment and really notice the love between you and the person you have chosen. Let it expand.

Is that easy? How easy? Do you find that resting in that love is easy and enjoyable? How easy?

Basking in love is wonderful, yet there is an even more enjoyable step to this game. Let's go on.

Finally, since you have easily noticed everything you did in the previous steps, we will expand our noticing even further.

Now I ask you to notice that this moment is happening, that this moment is underway right now.

Notice that it is Now, and Now is the only time there is. Simply notice that Now is what is in front of you and taking your attention.

Notice that it is Now.

Now is happening.

Things can be happening now. You can be reading this book now.

Maybe your nose is itching now, and you can still notice that Now is happening.

Maybe your nose is itching while you are reading this book, and it is all happening Now.

What is it like to notice Now?

I'll bet it takes no effort to notice that Now is happening.

You may notice that your gaze is a little diffuse as you notice Now. Perhaps your tongue is relaxed like a puddle in the back of your mouth as you notice Now. Maybe your whole body is relaxing while noticing Now.

I'll bet that you can still notice Now if someone is talking to you, or activity is going on around you.

Yet it is effortless to notice Now, that Now is happening. You do not have to strain to notice what is going on, because if you notice, simply notice Now, then everything is contained in the Now that you are noticing.

When you notice that Now is happening, and you effortlessly notice that things can be happening Now and let your attention be to the Now and not so much the things happening, then you are resting in Now.

You are in the state of least effort and most alertness, resting in Now.

Do you feel that? Is it easy?

1.9

More play with resting Now

Consider something you can notice when resting Now. When you are resting Now, and a judgment comes along, what happens?

If you examine this closely, you will see that no judgment can come from the outside because all around "just is."

It is YOU taking the input and making a judgment out of it. It is YOU pulling up a previous memory or experience and looking to see how it applies here and making a value judgment.

That judgment says that something could be some other way. Therefore, either it or you are wrong. They don't match — so something needs to change.

But what if you said, that's okay. That may be the way it is — in fact that *is* the way it is — because it came in that way.

So how could it be any different? Why change it? What would you change it to? The change would be arbitrary, because the past memory was arbitrary too.

The futility of persisting in a judgment is illustrated during a remodeling project in my home.

I had a vision of putting a door where I thought a door should be — separating the bathroom from the master bedroom. I ordered the door after taking measurements, and fitting it with my vision of how I wanted it to look. I wanted the door to go all the way to the ceiling, since that was the space that was open.

Then the workman came and started construction. I came home and saw a wall at the top of the opening and knew there must be a mistake. Then I re-checked the measurements of the door I ordered, and it was shorter than the space from the floor to the ceiling. The door I ordered was not what I originally wanted to order!

Immediately, I started wanting it to be different. It was agony thinking that I had wanted the door to be the full height, floor to ceiling, and I had ordered a shorter door.

I could not accept that the shorter door was what I had ordered, and what had arrived, and I clung to the idea of the taller door. But that was not the reality of it, so there was a huge conflict.

You may notice that the conflict was not what was in front of me; the workman was making the construction fit the smaller door.

The conflict was in ME, in wanting it to be different. What caused my suffering was hanging on to wanting it to be different, judging that it was not what I wanted, and wanting it to be what I originally wanted — a door spanning ceiling to floor.

When I finally let go of it, I saw how much pain I'd been causing myself by trying to make things different from what was right in front of me. It was painful to try to figure out how I had made the "mistake," and how I could send back the door and get the workman to pull out the wall.

Then I caused myself more pain trying to figure out reasons why the shorter door might be a better solution. I had to work it out in my mind for it to be okay. How silly!

Finally accepting exactly what was in front of me, even though it was not what I thought I wanted to be in front of me, brought me peace and rest from the mind.

I was finally resting in this present moment! That is what gave me peace. No longer did I wish I had done something different in the past. No longer did I punish myself for the order that I judged was a mistake. No longer was I projecting into the future to the installation of a door that I didn't want. It was all okay.

What was already happening, I accepted as okay. I was at peace with what existed in that moment. There was no more judgment about it. I noticed that being present in that moment, all that already existed was fine with me — and I would not change a thing.

Resting in the Now, it may happen for you that a memory comes up. When that memory comes up, it is most likely tainted by a charge of a judgment.

Focusing on the charged memory takes you right out of resting. Letting the memory pass by gently like a fluffy cloud on a summer day lets you stay resting in the Now. Resting is supreme.

Resting is a goal in itself that gives me the world. Resting in Now is my key to living a fruitful life. In my opinion, resting Now is the only worthwhile activity, if you could call it an activity.

Resting Now is the only thing there is in my world.

1.10

Resting is a feat, let's compete!

Resting is quite a feat! What is your ability to rest in this moment and only rest, simply rest?

There should be resting championships!

That would be a sight to see. Everyone gathered to rest and watch each other make no effort. Yet activity happens and interaction happens and yet everyone is resting.

Smack-down! The World RESTING Championships!

It is not a tournament of the lazy but a tournament of the focused.

The Champion Rester focuses on Now and only Now. The Champion Rester focuses on here and Now without effort.

The Champion Rester focuses in the Now, on this present moment, resting just here, now. Resting in this moment means staying here with no effort. She didn't spend any energy to get to the state of resting. Therefore, she puts out no effort in staying in the state of resting.

In fact, the Champion of all Champion Resters is able to rest back more in any moment. There is no end to the gentleness and easiness with which the Champion Rester can rest even more. The Champion Rester is infinitely resting!

You can tell a Champion Rester because there is a sense of contentment and ease that happens from resting in the Now. Yes, indeed, just resting.

You can be a Champion Rester. Don't complain you can't do it. Don't complain it's hard.

What could be easier than letting go and just gently resting back now?

Ahhhhh . . .

Resting in this moment, I notice relaxation and looseness in my body even though I am not checking in with my body to see if I am relaxed. It is one of the things I notice. I also notice that my mind is not chattering away. It is relaxed, too.

I notice things going on in the world, right in front of me, like a movie. I notice myself acting in the world, like a part of the movie. But I am not the star of the movie. I am flowing through the action in the movie, and it is simply happening.

There is a sense of flow and no effort, not thinking about what I am going to do next, not strategizing what is the best action to take. Each action arises in this moment, and it may be later that it makes sense in the big picture of my life.

I simply know and experience that everything is happening in the world to support me when I am resting. Everything happens to help me rest more and enjoy my life.

In addition, everything that happens, happens to support others when I am resting in this moment. Everything flows together for our mutual benefit when resting. The outcome is most assuredly better than I myself can think of, or than you can come up with by yourself. When resting, we allow the best to happen for all of us.

Remember the cold I had? While I was resting, I decided to allow more parts of me to rest, so I let go of the idea that I had a cold. I let go of the idea that it had to persist one moment longer. Then I let go into the resting Now, and allowed the awareness of the perfection of the moment to be the only thing in my awareness.

Later, my nose was clear and my face was no longer congested. Resting is supremely enjoyable, both in the moment and for what it brings.

1.11

Resting in a body

Life in a body can be a challenge if we are not resting in it, inhabiting it. There is a vital connection among the mind and emotions and body, so that each one vibrates to each other.

We talk about connection, but it really is of a whole. Resting in a body means inhabiting the whole.

When I was a teen, I did not think that you could not sleep without resting fully. I was surprised that when I went to bed, my back felt tight, and after a night of sleeping — which is the best form of resting that I knew about — I would wake up with my back still tight. How could that be, when I was resting?

At that time, I had no idea that my mind was not completely resting. When I was asleep, I had no conscious awareness, so I thought my mind was resting.

However, the day's accumulation of judgments and criticism that I personally accepted became stress that went into my mind. Some of it was processed during the night, during sleep, but some was stored in my mind — which, in effect, is throughout my body — causing tension.

Therefore, I was not able to rest completely from sleeping, because my mind still held the stressful tension of judgment and criticism exhibited in my body. I could not rest completely in my body because I was not resting completely in my mind and emotions.

At that time in my life, it was a challenge to be in my body. I was a teenager. The swirl of emotions and thoughts and ideas and concepts of who I was and who I needed to be was overwhelming.

I would bet you that I was not inhabiting my body fully. I resisted emotions, held onto thoughts in my mind and tried to make my body look different than it did. I was still getting used to having a body, mind and emotions! And it was constantly changing! What a challenge!

The challenge of life in a body can be met with resting in this present moment. Resting in this moment means inhabiting our body, inhabiting our mind and inhabiting our emotions. Resting involves inhabiting them all but not identifying with them.

Resting inhabiting the body is simply being aware of sensations, thoughts and emotions, and allowing them all to be there. It is resting in the awareness of what is flowing through the body.

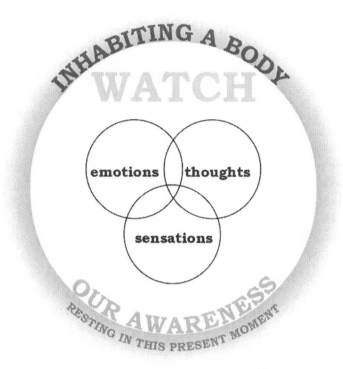

When we are resting this way, we notice the sensations but don't become them. We notice that thoughts and emotions go by but we don't become them. We notice that what we do makes a difference but we don't define ourselves that way.

Resting in this present moment, there is no judgment about the content or quality of the sensations, thoughts and emotions. It may be something our mind considers ugly, vile or painful, or perhaps something beautiful, soothing or righteous.

Either way, resting inhabiting the body requires letting them all go without judgment.

It is not our doing that brings the sensations, thoughts and emotions into experience initially. Therefore, there is no blame or credit to what appears. Resting, our job is simply to let them be. These sensations, thoughts and emotions will continue on out of our awareness as we notice them and let them be.

Resting inhabiting the body, there is no concern for the intensity of sensations, thoughts and emotions. There is only allowing them to be there. There is space and time for those sensations, thoughts and emotions to exist.

It is no use to push them away. Thoughts, sensations and emotions resist being pushed; they persist even longer, using energy from the push to stay around.

Besides, where would we push them *to*? There is nowhere else to go.

In this vast universe, sensations, thoughts and emotions appear in our awareness. Our awareness spans the universe, and there are no corners of the universe that are not part of our awareness. Therefore, there is no place to stash them; nowhere to tuck them away. They simply disappear from this universe — as easily as they came — when they are allowed to go.

Thoughts, sensations and emotions are allowed to go when they are not grabbed. They tend to come and go by themselves.

It is our attention on them, grabbing them, that makes them persist. However, if we allow them to be here, they go on their merry way. This is because when there is no attachment to whether they are there or not, they are free to disappear. If only you observe them flowing though, flow they will when they are not resisted or grabbed.

When I talk about grabbing a thought, it is that we follow the impulse to identify with the content of the thought and keep it around by grinding on it. "How *could* she do that? Well, I'll have to do this or that or the other to show *her*. What if she responds this way or that? That is the worst thing *possible*, unless . . ." — and on and on.

The natural consequence of grabbing one thought is that it generates more thoughts. Then there is a train of thought that takes us far away from this present moment.

Often one thought leads to imaginary conversations, redoing a situation so that I say what I wanted to say, or come up with a zinger. It could be in a meeting or a conversation in the future, fantasizing what I will say and the effect it will have. All sorts of scenarios that never will happen can be generated by grinding on the content of a thought.

Instead, letting each thought, emotion, or sensation pass by lets them do what they do naturally. They do dissipate as easily as they arose.

Each sensation, thought or emotion may be followed by another when they are treated this way. However, the next one can also be watched as if from a distance. Watching it means not owning it and making it your own, and not making it personal.

Watching thoughts, sensations and emotions is what we do when we are resting in this present moment. Resting and inhabiting all bodies — physical, emotional and mental — comes with being present now.

By noticing and resting in this present moment, we can be present to our body as well as to our mind and emotions. Resting in this present moment gives us rest of the body, rest of the mind, rest of the emotions. We rest in all of ourselves completely when we rest in this present moment.

Body, mind and emotions do not bother us as we rest in this present moment. Nothing can disturb the peace of this eternal moment.

Bad day/good day

Do you remember stubbing your toe on a day in which you were full of worry and anxiety? Most likely, that toe bothered you all day and made everything even worse.

You were grabbing the emotions of anxiety and worry, and the sensation of a stubbed toe, and making it personal, making it about you. You may have thought "Why did this happen to me?" "Why me?" "Why now, when I have to walk so far today?"

The result was that you were not resting in this present moment; you were not resting in what is; you were not resting in the totality of your spirit/body/mind.

You already were anticipating something, projecting to the future to worry and have anxiety about it. You were worrying about the meeting, or your performance, or the results of the test, or whatever was causing you worry. You were not resting in this present moment.

On top of that, this physical sensation, stubbing your toe, created even more suffering through grabbing thoughts such as "it's not fair that I stubbed my toe" or "this is making my day worse" or even more worry and anxiety. Those thoughts amplified the worry and anxiety.

Taking the event from the past, stubbing your toe, and projecting to the future and generalizing it, the thought of "My whole day is going from bad to worse" just compounds the suffering.

The sensation of your stubbed toe in the past is also taken from the past, labelled as pain, and projected into the future to cause suffering. "My miserable, aching toe!"

However, on a day when you were happy and carefree, stubbing your toe may not even hurt past the initial blow. That is the power of your mental and emotional state to influence your experience of pain.

You certainly noticed a sensation when you stubbed your toe on your carefree day. However, without labeling it, without grabbing it, without judging it as desirable or not, you did not experience it as pain.

By resting in this present moment, you are able to notice a sensation but not judge it — and so it passes. The experience of the happy and carefree day remains the predominant feeling.

In being happy and carefree, there was no thought of letting this sensation change that feeling. Without labeling the sensation, the happy and carefree state allowed the sensation to pass.

This is an example of resting in this present moment. It is the nature of feeling happy and carefree: to let all things pass without grabbing onto them. This state is key to allowing sensations to pass and not suffer.

In other situations, you have left resting and inhabiting your body when your focus of attention is only in the mind. Wrapped up in one thought as it leads to another, thoughts circle around and create worry and anxiety.

When you are totally absorbed in a mental process like trying to figure something out, remember the futility from my story of trying to figure out the situation with my friend, which I described previously.

When you are absorbed in a mental process, thoughts are often amplified with emotions such as fear and anxiety. In addition, thoughts escalate and swarm! For example, "Why did she do that?" "What was she thinking?" "Was it this or that?" "What will I do next time?" "What will happen if ...?"

Emotions add to the intensity of the mental focus and keep you out of your body. They keep you out of resting in this present moment.

The distraction of being totally mental or emotional, and not in your body can lead to clumsy actions, like bumping your head or stubbing your toe. You certainly were not resting in this present moment; your attention was in the mind or feelings.

In that case, it is a reminder to get back to embodiment by resting in this present moment. Instead of further ruining your day, you can use it to let you know that you were not present, and then rest again in this present moment now.

Resting in this present moment allows you to be present in your awareness and be present in your body.

Again, when you are present in your awareness, you are embodied. The way I see it, because the body is in your awareness, that awareness includes the awareness of the body.

The stereotype of the spacey New Age hippie is not an embodied person. If you have encountered a New Age hippie and interacted, you can distinguish that spacey state from rock-solid, present-moment awareness.

That spacey person may talk about expanded awareness and try to convince you that he is present. However, the spaceyness is from a disembodied concept of awareness, most likely. It could perhaps be a mental approximation or simulation of expanded awareness, and not actual awareness from resting in this present moment.

Once you have found the way to live in your body, inhabit your body, by totally resting in this present moment, you will never forget it.

In fact, you have always known it. You may purposely choose other places to put your focus, but you always will be able to choose to rest in this present moment.

The way that it happens for me to inhabit my body is while being aware of what is happening now in this present moment, I gently notice the still silent inner core of my being.

When I am resting here, in the core of my being, in this present moment, the sensation is one of deep relaxation. It is like a marble that has found the bottom of a bowl.

I feel what it feels like to rest at that place where gravity takes me, the place of least effort and most rest. There is no desire to go outward or upward, because the energy it would take is so tremendous. Attempting to leave is so filled with effort that it simply is not worth it.

Resting in the core of my being is an experience of stillness and absolute contentment.

Resting in the core of my being does not exclude anything around me; it precisely includes everything. That core of my being is everything — it is the universe inside me. Therefore, it includes everything.

Resting here allows me to notice the sensations in my body, and beyond that, to notice the world around. There is no limit to what I can notice from here. It is possible to notice all.

From this noticing of all, action arises. From the inside out, a response happens from my body and awareness which comes from the core of being. It is effortless and spontaneous. I notice it happening while resting.

Noticing from the core of being, as I described, will automatically let me attend to my body's needs. I eat when I am hungry. I sleep when I am tired. I choose activity appropriate to what my body and my life need.

Resting here and noticing automatically lets me respond in a way that is in alignment with who I am. It is a joyful way to live.

It is a way to live while being in the body, embodied, yet not being obsessed with the body.

It is a way to take care of the body in the way it wants to be cared for. It is using the wisdom of the body to know precisely what is up for attention now, whether it is being fed, getting sleep, stretching and moving, being social, or any variety of needs to be met. It is a natural and effortless way to live.

This is not an airy-fairy state of consciousness. Resting in this present moment does not turn me into a bliss ninny. In fact, resting in the present moment results in the most grounded, most alive state of being I have ever experienced.

I have gotten here bit by bit, and credit the practice of meditation both with my eyes closed and my eyes open. Using a tool, a technique, to return to this Now, over and over again, is my meditation practice. I have used this method to return to now again and again until I stay resting in this Eternal Now.

Once I became intimately familiar with the Eternal Present, recognizing that it has always been here, then I could rest Here by choice. Resting Here now is so attractive that the choice is a no-brainer. Resting Here happens by itself when I allow the Eternal Present to absorb my attention.

What I really am doing in returning to resting in this Present Moment is dissolving the stress in my nervous system that prevents me from experiencing the Now of this present moment. By resting in this Present Moment, stress dissolves by itself because it has no relevance to Now. Bit by bit distractions dissolve, leaving me a clear experience of resting in this Present Moment.

Resting here now is being present to what is arising in manifestation and being active in it. It gives me the most resources to bring to what is happening right now. It makes it the easiest to respond to what is happening for me right now.

By being present to what is here for me now, I see things as they really are. I see things without judgment or an emotional filter. I see clearly and allow this Present Moment to unfold with joy and serenity.

1.13

Judgment, emotions, action and rest

When I was in first grade, I overheard the teacher tell my mother that I was smart. I had a small idea about smartness and dullness, so that made an impression.

From then on, I identified with being smart, so I probably worked harder to prove it. Such a little thing so long ago has rippled into a big impact in my life.

Now "being smart" is something that I recognize has benefitted me but has also stood in my way. I pushed myself to get all A's because I was smart, and judged myself when I fell short. I did extra-credit work and was placed in advanced classes.

On the other hand, it has caused me to be okay with having not so many friends, because since I was smart, I liked to read books more than to go out with friends.

I began to dissolve all that by resting in the Now of whatever is. Smart, stupid, whatever.

Resting in this present moment, by definition, is resting in whatever is now. Not what I want to be now, not what I would rather have now, but what is actually here now.

If I said something stupid, then all right — I accept it and don't defend it. I can be stupid too. If I acted in a way that showed that I didn't know what was going on, then okay, I was stupid then too.

It doesn't matter because smart and stupid no longer define me. They both coexist in this body.

Smart and stupid are opposite sides of a coin. They are together in that coin, and as soon as I am one of them, it is possible to be the other. It doesn't matter. It really doesn't.

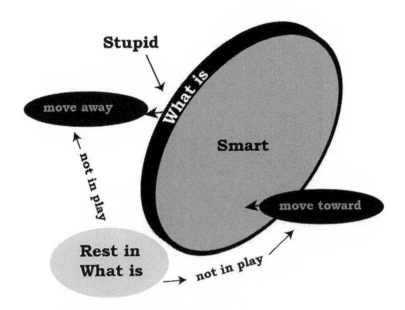

When I do not identify with being smart, I am not judging how smart I am in this moment, I simply am. In addition, it is not possible to judge myself as stupid in another moment.

When the coin of smart-stupid is not in play, neither side matters. Smart and stupid are both simply judgments, and resting in this present moment is beyond judgment. I know I can appear as either, if you are judging, but I do not identify with either.

By not taking on the judgment, by not having to identify myself as smart or stupid, I am able to remain resting in this present moment.

No rest with judgment

When judgment is absent, there is rest. When judgment is not in play, there is bliss.

If you think judgment is separating what is good from what is bad in order to go toward what is good and avoid what is bad, then I will show you another way.

Instead, consider allowing what is to be what it is. Allow everything to be exactly what it is as it is without evaluating it, judging it. Rest in the appreciation of what is without having to decide if it is something you need to approach or avoid.

Judgment is labeling something, and so it sets up mental and emotional activity to approach or avoid it. The mental and emotional activity takes us out of resting and takes us out of this present moment where our bliss is.

Without judgment, in a world of no good and bad, a world of no mistakes, there is only resting in what is, allowing what is to be what it is. And that resting is pure bliss.

There is no need to go towards something or avoid something else because resting brings exactly what is needed into life. Resting in this present moment brings only the best for our growth and further ability to rest in what is. It may not look like sweetness and light on the surface, but be assured, it brings us the experience of a sweeter life with more lightness if we let it.

Resting allows everything to come to us. We never need to go out towards or away from anything. We never need to chase anything. We never need to resist anything. What is here comes when we are resting. What is here is exactly what is called for right now. It is what feeds our bigger purpose.

Resting Now dissolves any lingering judgment, because there is no use for it. Judgment dissolves on its own because everything is fine in this present moment; everything is in its place. Everything is accepted for what it is.

No movement one way or another is necessary when resting. No movement is possible when completely resting in this present moment. Everything we need comes when we rest. Everything for the greatest good of everyone moves toward us when we are resting completely in this present moment.

When we are resting in the Now of this present moment, we are "Consciousness resting in itself." We are resting in our safe place, resting at Home. There is no other possible place to be.

Consciousness resting in itself can have no greater pleasure, because it is totally fulfilled. Resting by itself is fulfilling, just for its own sake. In addition, resting fulfills everything in life. Isn't it glorious that when resting, everything that comes is fulfilling!

Feelings and judgment

When we believe it is important to feel a particular way, then we set up judgments about whether what we are feeling matches that. We then fall into obsessively monitoring what we are feeling, then making a judgment about it.

We may judge that it is not okay to be angry, or sad, or too blissed out. When we feel those feelings, we may try to stop the feeling. From experience, I know that this doesn't work, and I hope you do too.

We don't have control over the feeling coming. We only have control over where we put our attention. And that influences whether the feeling stays. A feeling will stay around when we have tried to stop it, or unconsciously wallowed in it. We all have experienced wallowing in sadness. The sadness may have been in response to a circumstance, so we have no control over it initially happening. But when we notice the sadness, then is when we have the choice to follow it or to let it pass along.

Feelings will distract us from this present moment when we follow them. They can lead us into being immersed in the feeling without an awareness of this present moment. It is the difference between "I notice the feeling of sadness" and "I am sad." In the latter, we have identified with it and held onto it past its usual lifetime. We are wallowing in it. Feelings like sadness can stop us from doing something because we don't think we can do it with the feeling, sadness, there. The feeling overtakes our awareness and we cannot focus on anything else. But the feeling is there and gone when we don't hang onto it by identifying with it!

We certainly were a lot more like this as little children. If we were sad that we could not go to the birthday party, and were presented with a treat of our own, then the sadness was instantly redirected to joy in the treat. Because that was what was in front of us, and we were focused on what was in front of us, in this present moment. Emotions were fluid, and we were not weighted down with stuck feelings because we did not take them on as our identity.

While resting now, I am not concerned with what I might be identifying with; I am not checking into how I am feeling. I am filled with this eternal moment and checking into how I am feeling is a distraction. However, I may notice a certain feeling here, then notice it continue to move as another feeling comes. I notice the feeling as it is leaving, already moving along.

Checking in to a feeling takes effort and attention away from resting in this present moment. Besides, there is no sense of a "somebody" to check into! There is only this present moment. Resting right here, right now, completely fills up my entire awareness.

Now, in this present moment, judgment is absent. When I say or do something, I have no vested interest at all, for my identity, in how well I did as compared to a standard. Well, I may be curious for the fun of it and for growth. How I did does not ultimately affect my identity. My identity is immersed in this present moment. In any case, I totally accept what is happening, however it might be labeled. In fact, I am certain that it can be no other way.

Judging takes away from the knowing that things are exactly as they must be, and there is no other way they can be. Resting in this present moment, things are exactly as they are.

Resting Now, the judger is absent. The one who judges cannot exist Now! There is no need to stop judging when the one who judges is gone! What a simple solution. Just rest here now and judgment ceases!

All experiences

From resting here now, all varieties of experiences emerge. All experiences, from emotions to actions to understanding and mental processes, can be observed to emerge from resting right here, right now. These experiences emerge anyway, whether we observe them this way or not.

When all of these are experienced from resting, all is well. When all these are experienced from resting, things are in their right place. There is no need to change anything.

In addition, resting is the place of most creativity and productivity and usefulness in the world.

Resting in this present moment is the source of creation. It makes creation possible for us. It enlivens the creative process in the Now, where the future is unknown yet unfolding. It brings joys and creations previously unimaginable.

What more to life can there be than resting, because of what resting is and what resting brings?

If you want to be creative, rest in the all-potential of Now. After all, it is the source of creativity. Then, creating comes from the all-potential, and easily gives a solution or a combination of elements never previously imagined. There is immeasurable joy from creating from resting in this present moment.

If you want to be good in sports, rest in Now as you practice and play your sport. Indeed, action coming from the zero point of rest is the most dynamic. A muscle at rest can contract the farthest, doing the most work. If a muscle is already partially contracted, holding tension, then it has less potential to contract and will not propel a body forward as much as a muscle that was first at rest.

In addition, the precision of making a catch or hitting a ball is clearly done from that zero point of rest. That precision of being in the right place at the right time to connect with the ball comes from resting in this present moment. You may have experienced this, or seen it in the action of elite athletes.

If you want to be a mental genius, rest more fully in Now than in your mental concepts. To rest in Now is way beyond concepts, yet it can bring forth new ideas. Resting in this present moment is resting in the source of creativity, even mental creativity.

You don't need to manipulate concepts with your mind in order to be brilliant mentally. In fact, the greatest mental geniuses admit that their greatest discoveries came when they were not trying. They came at odd moments, when the mind as well as their whole being was resting, perhaps by being engaged in something trivial or sleeping.

It works. Ask any inventor or composer or star athlete. When they were in the zone in their sport, or had a flash of creative insight of invention or composition, they were resting.

Rest works. Rest is restful. Rest is pleasant.

Rest is being home, being at the home base where everything is possible and everything is manifested.

1.14

What removes us from resting

While resting, it is possible to notice thoughts and emotions. They are flowing through while we are resting. It doesn't matter that they are active and resting seems passive. When we let them all flow through, we don't let them disturb the peace of resting. In fact, active resistance to the thoughts and emotions increases their intensity, and stops us from resting.

When we notice a thought, and engage it, then we are no longer resting. When you notice a thought, let it go! Let it pass and don't engage it.

I promise you that you will be able to live without it! Resting shows us the way. Resting shows us that we can notice thoughts and not engage them. When we do not grab thoughts, we can rest more deeply in the moment where everything is done.

Thinking about resting also removes us from resting. It may be a habit to make what we are reading into an intellectual concept, but it will not free us from the mind.

To be free, all that is needed is to rest in this moment, now. Not thinking about this moment. Not thinking about resting in this moment. Simply resting without thinking.

We just walked through resting in this moment without thinking by noticing your hand, nose, back of your head, the space in the room, the space in a distant room, and the love you have for someone. When we notice that this moment is happening, we do rest in this moment happening now. This shows that we can simply rest now. And perhaps notice a thought or emotion — but rest supremely now.

Rest with emotions

When an emotion comes while resting, savor the flavor of it. This is life.

You may notice that the emotion is simply energy moving, and let your body and nervous system experience it now. That experience of now is what allows it to pass through while resting.

When we rouse from resting and grab that movement called an emotion and make it persist, then that emotion most likely will be experienced as too intense or painful. It is only the effortful act of moving out of resting that makes it an emotion that we don't want to experience.

It is easy to rest back into resting again. Once more, what is more effortless than resting? What is easy if not effortlessness?

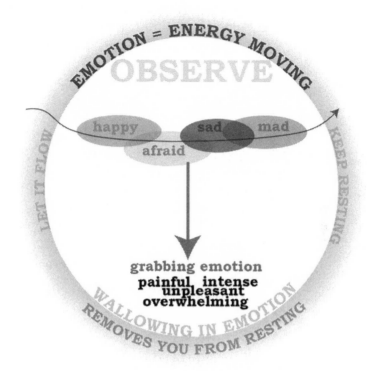

When dawn comes, the part of Earth resting in darkness notices the coming of the light. The transition of dawn breaking happens from rest with no effort. The light of dawn transforms the darkness, not clashing with it, not annihilating it. The Earth doesn't have to do anything to experience the dawn; it just happens. Then later, the darkness takes over again.

The movement of the Earth, spinning on its axis, doing what it does, brings the light and dark. Every place on Earth has no preference for dark or light. It sees both come and go with regularity. The light and darkness pass in alternation while the Earth is watching.

In the same way, when emotion arises, rest in now and notice that the emotion is movement. A light emotion comes while resting now. A dark emotion comes while resting now. Have no preference for the kind of emotion it is, just as the Earth has no preference for light or dark.

In fact, while truly resting, the emotion will only be movement. The perception of light or dark will not be a judgment resting in this eternal moment.

Resting allows for supreme enjoyment of emotion because it stays in Now and is effortless.

It is only emotion, locked onto and held beyond its natural duration, that is uncomfortable. Any emotion that is simply observed cannot be too intense or too overwhelming. It is only by resisting the movement of the emotion that creates the anticipation that it will be too much, too intense or overwhelming. By keeping the emotion at bay, we anticipate that it will be unpleasant. By wallowing in the emotion, we see that it becomes unpleasant. Approach emotion by noticing it as movement, and you will see that it is neither overwhelming nor unpleasant. Emotion flowing through is the stuff of life — and it becomes a joy ride while resting, no matter what the emotion.

Resting in Challenges

Challenges can be approached with resting as well. That is the farthest thing from what is obvious. I will show you that meeting challenges with resting is the most effective way.

Challenges could be characterized as something we have never done before, or something we have not dealt with before.

A challenge may appear when we are asked to do something that seems contrary to our personality. But in that case, it is contrary to our personality, our conditioned nature, what we have become accustomed to believe is us.

The challenge can be to do something a little better, a little more — to develop our skills, in order to stretch and grow. It might be to settle more deeply into who we really are — our true nature — and express it.

When something may seem challenging, we want to cringe and avoid it because the part of us that has been conditioned to be a certain way is being pressed to go beyond its limitations. The concept of ourselves, which is a limited concept – I'm not an artist, I can't talk to people, I'm not good at the business side of it – whatever is the repeated refrain that goes through our head when presented with a new situation – is what is being challenged.

On another level, it is the part of ourselves that chooses that is being challenged to go for growth instead of listening to those thoughts that tell us that we are not up to the challenge. The chooser is faced with those thoughts that tell us that we are not up to what we are being asked to do. The natural conclusion from those thoughts is that we cannot possibly meet the challenge.

That part of us that chooses, fortunately, has a guiding light. By being guided by our deepest desires, the part of us that chooses can put a challenge into perspective. Being in touch with our highest desire, that thing that makes everything else worthwhile, is very important in life.

If you could boil down your wishes to only one that encompasses everything that would fulfill you in life, what would that be? What is your highest desire? I shared that previously the one thing for me was "peace." Now I feel more drawn to "enjoyment" as my highest desire. For others, it is "love" or "purpose." What is that one highest desire you wish for yourself?

With that one highest desire in mind, the part of us that chooses has to go for what we really want. When we know what we really want, how could we not choose for it, no matter what the challenge? When that part of us that chooses is rooted in knowing who we really are –

unlimited instruments of manifestation of our highest desires – that choice is easy; it is a no-brainer.

Literally, it takes no intellectual smarts to choose what we are already, and to choose for it now. It takes no weighing the pros and cons, no debating the cost with the outcome, no work at all from the mental or even emotional level.

That part of us that knows who we are will always go for being more of who we are by making the choice to go for our highest desires.

In being faced with a challenge, there may be a moment of recognition that this is something new and more skills can be developed for it. With it comes the sensation of stretching for growth. In addition, there may be the recognition that this is something for which our skills are not developed enough to meet the challenge at its level, and the skills will be developed by meeting the challenge.

Whatever the situation, from this point of view the answer is always a hearty "yes – bring it on!" That is because the choice has come from the heart, which knows there is always more. It is our birthright to expand to being more. This is especially evident when the mind does not see there is any more and has put a limitation on growth. The heart knows our highest desire, and overrides the objections of the mind. The no-brainer decision comes from the heart's knowing.

Even though I did not like getting up in front of a group, I volunteered to do a presentation in a professional setting. My approach was to prepare in the ivory tower of my mind, work out what I wanted to say, and the flow of it, and put it into a Power Point presentation. Then all I had to do was read the Power Point in front of people to successfully get through the presentation. From the comments I got later, I realized that was not the way to do it. They were bored. They did not need me there reading it.

I loved consolidating ideas, especially about wholeness and wellness, and bringing out a message. But presenting the message so that people connected with it, and got it, was another story. This is an example of a challenge in which I did not have the skills to meet the situation at the time. By doing the presentation, I got powerful feedback that I needed to build my skills.

Since then, I have joined Toastmasters to build my skills in communication, public speaking and leadership. It was an impulse from my heart, since in front of a group is one of the very few places where I could not maintain resting in this present moment.

Public speaking was not something I thought I wanted to do, because it went against my introvert personality. Public speaking was not something I had much experience in, so it was relatively new to me. Therefore, in two ways it was a challenge.

I started public speaking with nervousness, checking notes, and haltingly expressing myself in words. By approaching it as building a skill, I was okay with that. I knew I was following my highest desire to express myself in front of a group while resting in this present moment.

It was a challenge to acquire the skill of public speaking. As a skill, it was something I could develop bit by bit. It was something at which I could get better gradually. It was a challenge I was up for. My heart was directing me to do it.

With practice, I am building the skill of speaking in public while resting in this present moment. It is actually the only way I can effectively speak in public.

While building that muscle of preparing speeches and speaking while being present, I am building the skill of speaking in public effectively.

1.15

Resting, Alertness, Thoughts

There are certain aspects of resting in this present moment that may seem contrary to our experience.

We may experience rest as a state of blurred awareness, letting down the guard of the mind and letting it all hang out. Rest may feel like grogginess, or the mind on vacation. Rest may be vegging out, zoning out, not being conscious of anything. Rest may be the experience of blotting out consciousness as in sleep. We may equate resting with being a couch potato, being entertained and letting the body go horizontal.

That is not the rest of resting in this eternal moment. It may seem strange, however, that true rest in this present moment brings alertness.

I'll say it again. Resting here, Now, brings alertness.

There is no effort in this alertness because it comes from resting now. Since there is no effort, we can notice with clarity what is here in this present moment. Since rest does not interfere with what is, we can see what is right here in its purity with no distractions.

Now, the body may have to get some restorative sleep and rest before it can experience much of the alertness of this present moment. While resting, we mobilize detoxification and repair, so there is a lot of movement while resting. When there is no longer a huge backlog, then we can rest without an excessive amount of that restorative movement. Then it is easier to really rest, and in so doing, to be alert. At any rate, we can experience alertness with rest in this present moment any time, as long as we can stay 100% present.

If you do not experience this, you may not be deeply resting in this present moment. You may be wrapped up in sensations, emotions or thoughts. You may be noticing the fleeting moments, not the eternal moment of Now. Or perhaps it could be because there is a subtle belief that this is not true for you.

Athletes know and experience alertness, vibrant aliveness and resting when they are peak performing. In order to run at top speed, the mind and the body must be at complete rest, using only the required muscles. Not only do the muscles have to be resting when they are not used, the mind has to be resting to be alert.

Peak-performing athletes fundamentally rest, while alert to the body's and mind's actions in that moment. They are completely alert to their surroundings. To be completely at rest and completely in action, competing, is exhilarating! Athletes crave their sport because of the moments of vibrant aliveness they feel.

Artists and all people engaged in creative activity know this as well. By resting in this moment, I am alert to the creativity of the moment coming from being present. This creativity is not jumping ahead to see what is being created. It is perfectly resting right now being alert to see, hear or feel what wants to be created coming forth in this moment.

It is as if I am watching the creation form in front of my eyes. I, as an artist, am resting in the creative process. I am swept up with the action of creation while resting, watching, alert to and enjoying what happens.

Artists love creating, because we feel totally alive in the process.

You can verify this when you are resting completely in the present moment. Whatever comes of this moment comes because you are alive and the moment is alive. You are alert to what is here while you are resting here.

In fact, resting and alertness are directly proportional.

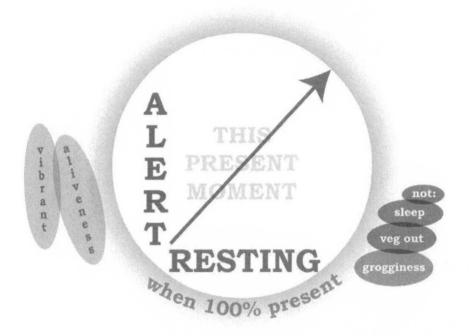

The more I rest in this present moment, the more alert I am to this moment. I am alert to what is coming to me and what opportunities are here. I am alert to the pristine stillness in this present moment.

Have you seen a forest animal watching its surroundings? It is completely alert to what is going on in the environment. In order to do that, it must be relaxed and resting.

I've seen bunnies munching grass and alert to me approaching. I have been struck that they are completely at rest in doing so, even if they are ready to run in the next moment.

It's the strategy of "Wait for it — wait for it."

When resting while alert to what is going on, there is no need for tension or movement until the moment when the situation alerts them that escape is needed now. It is relaxation that allows for the alertness to be attentive to the moment.

Alertness is also attentiveness.

When I am attentive to my mind, I let the thoughts come and go without grabbing them to identify with them. This is the attentiveness of resting in the present moment.

When I am attentive to what this moment is bringing me, I am resting right here, right now. I am attentive to this moment and not what my mind may be producing.

Being attentive to what is here in my experience may sound like it takes a great deal of energy. The truth is quite the opposite.

It takes a great deal of energy to hang on to beliefs and follow thoughts. How much energy does it take to grab onto a heavy object and hold it in front of you? The longer you hold it, the more tired you get, because it takes lots of energy.

Alternatively, how much energy does it take to put down the heavy object and let go? In the same way, it takes no energy to simply let thoughts flow by.

When I let thoughts arise and dissipate, it allows my mind to rest. Then I experience the mind as pristinely alert. I experience alertness without thoughts as vibrantly alive and brimming with potential.

I experience life itself, ready for whatever is being created. Life living life. Life living me.

There is innocence in this alertness because it is only focused on this moment. The innocence comes from not jumping ahead to suppose what a future moment holds. The innocence comes from not hanging on to what happened in the past and thinking it will happen again. The alertness of this moment lets things unfold as they do, without wanting it to be different.

The alertness is pure in its innocence.

I remember a time when I was struggling to experience the alertness of this present moment. I heard that it came from resting. However, when I thought that I truly indeed was resting in this present moment, there was fuzziness. From that fuzziness, I tried hard to be alert. It simply was not my experience.

You can see my dilemma! Trying is the opposite of resting.

When I looked closely at it, when I was alert and attentive to my experience, I realized that I had a subtle belief. This belief was based on thoughts that this was not true for me. That fuzziness came from the thoughts and belief held in place that I could not experience alertness in this present moment.

The moment that I saw that I was believing the thought that I could not experience alertness, that thought dissolved.

At the moment the thought disappeared, I experienced a tingling in my head that I associate with "aha." The thought and belief dissolved just like that when I looked at them face-on. It took seeing that the thought was there to face it.

The result was that I indeed am resting in this present moment with alertness.

From this, you may be able to see that being present is the opposite of entertaining thoughts. The more we entertain thoughts, the less present we can be to this moment.

Thoughts agitate us and distract us and take us out of resting in this present moment. Thoughts reminisce about the past and have anxiety for the future. The more we are able to see our thoughts as something flowing through the clear space of the mind, the more easily we can choose not to entertain them. We can choose to allow them to keep going, dissipating after arising.

When we allow that to happen, observing with alertness, the thoughts dissipate without any energy or effort. There is no resistance to thoughts while resting in this present moment.

If this seems a bit foreign, then perhaps you might want to use a tool or technique to bring you to this Present Moment and watch carefully for thoughts. That is how I started. While purely resting Now, I notice the clear background of the mind, and there are some spaces without thoughts.

I am fascinated by the experience of resting in this present moment, and noticing thoughts as they start to arise. Being so very attentive, I can catch a thought as it arises, before it becomes fully formed. It is like a wisp of movement. I am not even aware of what the thought might be about.

The more I rest, the more alertness I experience. The more alert I am, the less I care about thoughts arising.

The more deeply I rest in this present moment, the more my attention goes to the stillness and fullness of this moment, and not to any thoughts arising. The fullness of this present moment is so engaging that I don't care if a thought arises or not.

Thoughts arising can never disrupt our ability to rest in this present moment. When we are resting in Now, thoughts arise and dissipate all by themselves. It is resistance to thoughts, and belief that thoughts need to be cleared from the mind in order to be in this present moment, that further fortify thinking.

If you make it a matter of a battling against thoughts, you have already lost. You can never push thoughts away. You can never stop thoughts from coming. They are simply movement in this universe of blinking.

The grand irony is that when we allow thoughts to be here, they dissolve on their own. When we allow what is movement to move, it will do so. What is left is the simple innocence of this present moment.

Allowing and not engaging is the gentle way to deal with thoughts. Not caring if there are thoughts moving through is the way to freedom.

There are techniques which make this simple in the beginning. My tendency was to use a thought to get rid of a thought. But that led to continued thinking! However, there are thoughts which are powerful tools to bring us to this Present Moment. When I learned and used these tools, everything became simpler. Resting Now, thoughts dissolve. There is no battle! We are left in peace.

Resting in this present moment is never accompanied by a sense of boredom. There is such alertness filling this present moment that it can never be boring. The stillness, the gentleness, the alertness of this present moment engages me completely as I rest here.

If we perceive an activity to be boring, it is because we have left resting in this present moment. A comment on the experience arises, saying that it is boring. Or our thoughts stray, and we believe a thought that says being somewhere else, doing something else, would be more interesting. When we believe that comment and don't see it as a thought floating through, then boredom can exist. We have grabbed the feeling of boredom and identified with it, resulting in being bored.

Whatever we are focusing on is our apparent reality, or experience, for the moment. If we are focusing on boredom, then that is our experience.

If our focus is this present moment, resting here, then the experience we find will never be boring. The experience is aliveness, alertness, and attentiveness.

1.16

Gentleness and Stillness and Compassion

Resting in this present moment automatically brings gentleness and stillness. They are qualities of resting.

In addition, the more gently I approach my experience, both with myself and those around me, the more Stillness I experience as the pervading basis of that experience. This Stillness provides the context in which everything else is experienced.

It is this rock-solid stillness that allows gentleness. Just a whispered impulse, arising from that which does not move, generates the gentleness of a slight movement. The Stillness is the source, and what it creates is the world where we live. We live in the realm of movement, but our source and the stuff of this movement realm comes from Stillness.

I experience that being based in Stillness allows an ease of living. The ease comes from not needing to work things out, not needing to force things, not needing things to be a certain way. The ease is from letting things unfold from the Stillness, the source that needs no direction.

To live in gentleness is to act from the Stillness. Since a gentle movement is such small movement originating from rest, it retains a lot of the qualities of resting.

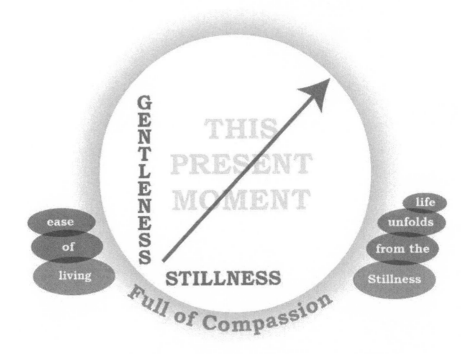

Living in gentleness is living from resting in this eternal moment. Acting from the Stillness brings gentle acts. It brings with it the Stillness, and even compassion. An action from the Stillness is full of compassion.

Compassion allows our interactions to be in the best interest of ourselves and those with whom we interact. With the wisdom of the Stillness, the source of all being, and the ability to relate to others from our own human experience, we can act with compassion.

Resting in this present, eternal moment, I am at one with everything in this moment. I am one with my surroundings and the people here. I am one with the loving intention of the universe. Acting with the knowledge and wisdom of the oneness, I act with compassion.

When I rest in this present moment, I experience the universe within me.

Resting in this present moment, you will also experience that everything in this universe is within you. The boundary between me and the world dissolves. The boundary between you and the world dissolves. The boundary between you and me dissolves. The boundary was never real in the first place.

When I realized that the whole universe is here, while I rest in this present moment, I realized that resting in this present moment affects everything in this universe. It affects me and it affects you and since the whole universe is within us, it affects the whole universe. Resting in this present moment is the biggest way to affect the whole universe.

Resting in this present moment may simply bring contentment. We may not realize the impact it is having on the universe.

However, in our interactions in our daily life, we may begin to appreciate the effect it is having on the whole universe. Store clerks are delighted to serve us. Waiters are more attentive and gracious. Even traffic parts for us when we are resting in this present moment.

Resting in this eternal present is the way to act compassionately in the world. We don't have to be Mother Teresa with a life dedicated to serving. Simply by resting Now, we are resting in the source of compassion. Simply resting here, in this eternal moment, we know that our every act is compassionate.

We are here now. We are compassion resting here, Now. There is no other time to be in this present moment. There is no other time to be than in this present moment.

We are in the habit of being distracted from this beautiful, eternal moment. However, once we learn to let thoughts, emotions and sensations come and go, this present moment is experienced as all-pervasive. Now is the only time there is.

Alertness, innocence, gentleness, stillness and compassion are here now. Are you?

1.17

Our natural state vs. suffering

It may not be readily apparent from our experience that our natural state is to be present.

I now know that resting in this present moment is our default state. I know from experience that it must be our natural default state because it takes so much effort to leave resting here. It is such a bother to think and identify with feelings. The freedom of this present moment and what happens when resting here has to be what is naturally ours.

You may not believe this if you constantly experience chatter in your mind. You may not believe this if you are depressed or anxious. You may not experience rest, ease and enjoyment as a default state.

However, when you have, and do, and will experience, even if for a moment, resting in this present moment, there is so much relief! The relief is as palpable as walking off a busy street into a quiet spa. It is as palpable as taking off sticky, stinky, too-tight, uncomfortable clothes. It is as palpable as what it feels like to stop poking yourself with a sharp stick.

The rest of this present moment is the antidote to the busy mind. It is the antidote to being wrapped up in feelings. It is the antidote to being miserable.

I know that this is a radical perspective for most of the world. However, feeling within, you can know that this is how things are. You know it is true when you stop and rest.

When you allow thoughts to come and go, you are resting in this present moment. When you let emotions come and go without grabbing them, you are resting in this present moment. The emotions and thoughts are movement, and to stop the flow of that movement is to create another movement called suffering.

Suffering is simply stopping the flow of movement. It is grabbing onto a thought, emotion, or sensation and believing it is truly who you are. That act confines you to a single experience, not allowing you to be the experiencer.

You would never make that mistake with a costume, would you? You would not put on a pirate costume and believe that you are a pirate. Wearing a Halloween costume of a cat does not make you a cat, does it?

In the same way, don't make that identification with an emotion, thought, or sensation. When you notice an emotion, or thought, or feel a body sensation, notice it without identifying with it. The stakes are much higher with these than with Halloween costumes. Once you wear thoughts, feelings, or sensations as your identity, you suffer.

What this looks like in real life is simple to see. Stop and watch what is going through your awareness. As you feel, think or sense, stop and watch. Make some distance between you and what you observe. Take time to simply observe.

When you are immersed in a feeling, it has covered you like a costume. There is no distance between you and the feeling. You don't even know who you really are because you think you are the costume. You think you are the feeling. Your immersion in the feeling has distracted you from who you really are.

Instead, take the costume off and look at it. That means look at the emotion as if it wasn't yours. Make distance between you and the emotion.

Take a good look, and in so doing, you will recognize that if you can watch it, the emotion being watched is not the watcher. The thing watched, the emotion, is not you. The emotion that you can watch is energy flowing through you.

It may be attractive to be in the emotion because it gives you an adrenaline rush or a dopamine reward. Perhaps it matches what you think you should feel; your feeling is appropriate to the situation. Perhaps you feel righteous to have that feeling. You deserve to feel this way, considering the circumstances.

Those justifications about the emotion in which you have immersed yourself are not useful to listen to. The attraction of being in the feeling and not watching it will lead you away from this present moment. Any more thoughts and feelings about the feeling in which you are immersed will further lead you astray.

Those thoughts and feelings justifying the first thought and feeling are more costumes, more things that are not you. They are generated by the original mis-identification — you being the costume — and are like more-detailed accessories added to the costume that you already have on. The pirate has a patch over his eye. He has a sword by his side. That makes him more convincing as a pirate. He must be a pirate. No mistake.

However, the reality is that none of that is you. You are compounding your mistaken identity. You are not the costume or what it correlates to as the thought or the feeling.

In addition, physiological processes are continuously going on in your body. You are digesting, filtering blood, exchanging oxygen for carbon dioxide, mobilizing white blood cells, responding to the environment and what is perceived there, and much more. These physiological processes may generate thoughts, feelings, and sensations.

To respond to them as useful information is misleading. Just because you ate a heavy meal which is hard to digest, you may get a headache and feel angry. This is a cloak of anger put on your real self, and it has nothing to do with those around you or your life. Take the cloak off and look at it. It is the cloak of anger. It is not you. To wear it, you suffer. To see it as a costume that you can take off liberates you. You know who you really are: the one who notices the emotion.

Feelings spawned by thoughts are not useful to follow either. Having the thought that "This is not going my way" can be compounded by the feeling that I am a loser; I am lonely and sad. These too are embellishments to the original costume that you put on. They compound the distraction from the truth of this present moment.

Neither body sensations nor emotions are useful feedback compared to what you can glean from resting in this present moment. In this eternal moment, this present, all is well. Now, there can be thoughts and emotions passing through, but they can be entertaining costumes. Or perhaps you notice them moving through and don't even notice what kind of costume it is. The real you is what was here before the costumes came along. You are what is underneath when you put the costume on. You are what is left when you take the costume off. You are that thing that does not change and cannot be touched, and all is well.

Fortunately, resting in this present moment gives you the way to remove the costumes if you have put them on. Also, it gives you the way to avoid putting on the costume to begin with.

Resting in this eternal moment gives you the perspective that thoughts, feelings and sensations are costumes, no different than dressing up as a pirate. Resting Now shows that there is choice about having them on and taking them off. There is a choice of resting now or identifying with the costume you have put on. You are not the pirate. You are the one observing the pirate costume.

There is always a choice of taking off the costume when you notice you are wearing it, identifying with it. You can take it off. When you notice that you have taken on a thought as if it were true, then rest in this present moment. That is how you take it off. When you feel wrapped in emotions, then rest back in this present moment. When you feel body sensations, believing that they are you, then rest back in this present moment.

If you are often wrapped in emotions or body sensations, then you may want to use a tool or technique to be able to rest back into this Present Moment. Just resting back may seem too hard to do, but a tool makes it easier.

When you are able to rest in this present moment, the thoughts, emotions and sensations you had thought were you show themselves obviously to not be you. You can see them as costumes you had identified with for a time.

Resting in the Now of this eternal moment, you can see you are the one underneath the costumes. You notice that you can see the costumes being offered to you, and you do not have to put them on and become them. Under no circumstances do you have to keep them on.

Make resting in this present moment more important than thoughts, feelings or sensations. Make knowing who you are more important than the things moving through your experience. When you do that, you have the antidote to suffering.

Most likely, you will need help in doing this. After becoming familiar with seeing and watching the thoughts, feelings, and sensations flowing through your experience, then you have a choice about what to do. There are tools to instantly, reliably take your attention to this present moment. By practicing, you can become familiar with this present moment and experience its benefits. By getting guidance to illuminate your blind spots, you can rest more and more in this eternal moment.

You then can use tools to bring your attention back to this eternal moment when you notice you are wrapped in thoughts and emotions or sensations. Your choice is like noticing you have a costume on, then being able to take it off. It is a simple choice.

Making this choice relieves you from suffering. It relieves you from ever having to experience any more suffering. When you use this choice, you rest in this present moment where there is no suffering.

Remember, resting in this present moment is easy because it is your default state. It is the "you" underneath the costumes. It is you, naked and pure. It is you, in joy and peace and love.

The costumes of thoughts, feelings and sensations are things flowing through our experience. They are here to enjoy as long as they keep moving along, which is their nature.

We can enjoy them as beautiful costumes, as long as we don't put them on and think we have that identity. We can delight in the pirate costume or the cat, all the while knowing that they are not us, but flavors of experience.

Therefore, thoughts, feelings and body sensations are not the real you. The emotion worn as your real self is a hollow mock-up for the real you. You are so much beyond that costume that you are kidding yourself every time you think you are the costume. Resting in this present moment shows you this.

1.18

The highest form of prayer

Resting in this present moment, in this Infinite Now, is the highest form of prayer. It is a pleasure to be so of service in any moment that we simply rest here. It is a pleasure to be so connected, immersed, identified and able-bodied, wholly and holy.

In this eternal moment, there is no separation between what is prayed about and the one who prays. There is the one who prays, the pray-er, the act of praying, and the object, prayer. Even our words identify the one who prays, the prayer, as the same word as the object, the prayer.

When the subject, object and activity all collapse into one thing, there is only the One of this present moment. That gives incredible rest because we are not leaving our true nature, the true identity of who and what we are. When we do not leave who we are, there is no energy expended. Therefore, it is completely resting and restful.

The highest form of prayer is resting in the Infinite Now, which is an affirmation of all there is, of all you are, and of all that could be. In this eternal now, we are consciousness resting in ourselves. That is the source of all abundance, balance, and growth. What more could we pray for?

From this resting point of view, that is, resting in Now, all creation happens. All creation happens from this very moment, this present moment, and everything is created new. In this new creation, there is the opportunity to have a fresh perspective. As creation is arising ever new, in this eternal moment, it automatically is fresh. That perspective of a new creation is of creation identified with the Creator.

With that self-identity, nothing can be out of place. Nothing can be wrong. Nothing, no-thing is the self-identity. As the perspective is not identified with any THING, it is able to be of everything and nothing at the same time.

This is prayer in its highest form. It is the prayer of the pray-er who is resting in this present moment. It is the highest form of being in this world. It is the most beautiful, most fulfilling, most joyful way of being in this world.

By praying without ceasing, the pray-er is resting in this Infinite Now, continuously, and only in this present Now. This Now is the eternal present. It is only Now.

Not the now that is between the past and the future, but the Now that contains everything and can be our single point of focus. It is the Now that was never created, but that exists before creation, and beyond creation. Now contains everything in creation as well.

In contrast, when we leave resting in Now, in this eternal moment, when we cease praying, we have made our priority something less than we truly are. We have decided that it is more important to worry or be anxious than to rest in the glory of creation.

In this case, it is evident that we have engaged learned patterns of behavior that do not trust the complete rest of this eternal moment. We have learned to go to the past and feel guilty, regretting what happened, or go to the future and feel anxiety about what might happen.

When you see one of these patterns emerge, when you become present and aware of it, you have a choice.

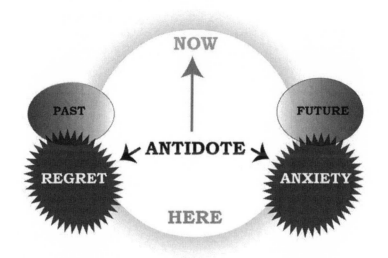

You can choose to feel regret or worry, and make that choice more important than resting in this present moment. It may feel like it is more important because it is what we are familiar with, what we know.

Or you can choose to rest in this eternal moment. The habit of worry or regret can be abolished by simply resting in Now, resting in this Infinite Now.

By choosing to regret or be guilty, or to worry and be anxious, we are saying that we don't trust what this present moment brings. We have to take control because there is the possibility that it will not turn out right.

When we feel guilty and regret the past, it is because what happened was not perfect for all concerned. For what happened to be a mistake, life was not unfolding perfectly.

If things went wrong, they went wrong according to what your perception of what should happen would be, not what actually unfolded. For in this present moment, the experience is of perfection. The experience is that nothing is out of place and nothing is missing. When our perception is not aligned with this, we can draw all sorts of conclusions.

We do sometimes take a stand and believe that evil happens in this world and get upset with the Creator. We get angry with the Creator and believe that we could do it better. We think that our little perspective would be able to do things better, because we don't think what actually happened was serving us.

In this little perspective, we don't see the big picture that the Creator knows and is. From our limited perspective, we think things should go a certain way, and we don't see the consequences beyond our little perception of the world. We are blind to what is possible.

We can't possibly know where we are headed in this world of experience. Our perspective is too limited. Creator has the omniscient and infinitely compassionate perspective.

We don't need to trust in the Creator. Trust is not necessary, or even possible, in this present moment. Trust implies a belief in something and the willingness to count on it coming through for us.

Belief is not necessary when we are resting in this present moment. While resting here, we are experiencing the wholeness, the completeness, the rightness of this eternal moment. There is no doubt resting here.

There is nothing to trust because all doubt is erased, leaving only the knowingness that all is well, all is right with the world. There is nothing to believe because in this present moment lies complete certainty that all is well.

When we are not resting in this Infinite Now, we are asleep to what is. We are living the definition of being asleep; we are not consciously conscious. We are distracted by thoughts, beliefs and misperceptions about ourselves and the world.

Resting Now, we dispel all those misperceptions. We can see what is, and we see it clearly. It is as if we have woken up, the dreamy world of sleep that we believed was what was happening is gone, and we have opened our eyes to see.

Living in this moment is all about being consciously conscious so that we can fully participate in this wonderful world. We can be awake and aware to participate in it and easily, joyfully, play our part.

We don't have to be consciously aware of how we fit in this world. We simply rest in this present moment. What is here for us is presented to us in this moment. All we have to do is engage it, playing fully.

Resting in Now gives us the alertness and awareness to play. In playing our part, we get to rest even more, knowing nothing is wrong and out of place. We get to enjoy our lives thoroughly.

I find the ultimate fulfillment in resting in this present moment, which I experience as eternal.

It is the fulfillment of who I am. It is the fulfillment of what I want to do in this world. It is the fulfillment of my desires, seeing them manifested as gifts coming to me almost as a surprise.

It is the fulfillment of seeing a world around me that I want to live in. It is playing with the people here in this present moment that gives me joy and fulfillment.

I used to think I was a dreamy idealist, not wanting to live in this world. Resting in this eternal moment gives me everything I always wanted and knew somewhere deep inside I could have. Resting here now is living in this world. It is the fulfillment of living the life I always wanted to live.

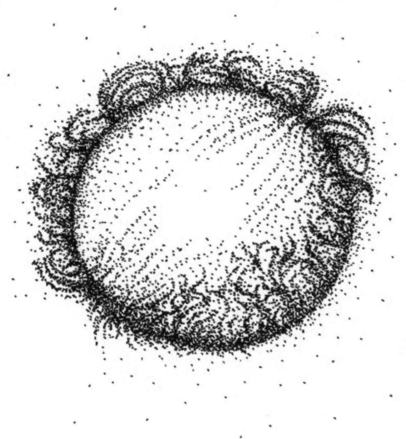

II.
The world we create
resting in this eternal present

The Golden Universe

When we are resting in this present moment, perfectly resting in the infinity of now and being fully alive and engaged in what is being presented to us in this moment, then we are creating a different world. We are living in a Golden Universe! It is alive and active in itself through us.

We can recognize the different way of operation of this Golden Universe by the principles by which it functions. These principles are what are operating by the Golden Universe simply being itself. As the Golden Universe is within us and encompasses us, we are the Golden Universe in completeness.

These principles are not hard to understand. They are the simplest thing to see, because they are our nature!

Being our nature, they are the easiest things to discover. They are also easy to maintain because they happen by themselves while we rest in this present moment.

Following these principles is the easiest thing to do. Look at it this way: The nature of the Golden Universe is our nature. We can't NOT follow them, naturally.

We know these principles so deep in our being that we don't have to be told what they are and how to follow them.

Nevertheless, some of us may persist in wanting to rebel and not accept that these principles are operating. That can only happen from a state of effort. It is the effort of being somewhere else besides resting in this present moment.

When we are no longer resting in this eternal moment, then we leave the Golden Universe. We return to the familiar world of suffering and strife.

That happens when we make the humongous effort of moving out of this present moment to chew on something from the past. Or make the ginormous effort to worry about the future. It may not seem such a gargantuan effort to go back or forward, because we have been doing it all our lives and are used to losing a lot of energy. Whichever way we go, back or forward, it is our old programs still operating that make these other concerns more important than right now.

Because we have made them most important, they take our whole awareness. We lose sight of the Golden Universe. We are immersed in thought, over and over: why I was right, why he was wrong, what will we do next? We are immersed in emotion, regret for the past and worry for the future. Most likely we are feeling physical pain as well.

You may not currently perceive being immersed in the old programs as requiring a lot of effort. That is simply because they are your habit. You have the habit of letting your attention be drawn to the past or future because of the strong emotion or programming that is operating out of your awareness. Were you to be aware and rest in Now, you would feel the effort it takes to leave the Now.

It is possible to be relieved of the effort of following the programs of the past, and rest in this present moment, observing these principles and watching the Golden Universe be created.

The programs may have told you that to get ahead, you must do more. That is why you didn't balance activity with rest. You may have believed that you could not be yourself; that you have to censor or modify who you are. Once you decide not to follow those old programs, though, you have the opportunity to rest in these natural principles. You have the opportunity to rest again in this present moment.

The decision to no longer follow those old programs starts with being attentive to what is operating. When we see what is operating, we have the chance to not choose the programmed behavior by choosing instead for resting back into this present moment.

There is always the opportunity to rest here, Now. There is always that opportunity when we are aware of it. The old programs have distracted us from this opportunity. Now that old program, doing the same things from the past over and over again, can become a trigger to make a different choice.

We can choose to rest in this present moment, especially when we have a tool to do it easily.

Rest in the Principles of this Golden Universe

You most likely will recognize what I am about to describe. These principles are self-evident from my experience of resting in this eternal moment, and I believe they will be to you too.

When you read the following descriptions, you are bringing these principles to awareness.

Next, you can notice them in action and then reinforce them in subsequent action. This is not by any effort or concerted mental discipline, but by resting in this present moment.

Perhaps you notice when you are not following them because you feel out of balance and something is not working in your life. That leads to pain and suffering if it continues. You have left the Golden Universe.

Being aware of these principles is an excellent opportunity to end the pain and suffering with what is not working in your life. You can regain and maintain balance by simply resting back into this present moment.

Principle 1: Be Yourself

The first Principle of the Golden Universe is to BE YOURSELF, simply and naturally. By your very nature, you are yourself. If you are not yourself, who will be you? Who else is there to be?

That question popped up in the 2004 film *I ♥ Huckabees*. It is about a couple who helps others solve their existential issues, the kind of issues that keep people up at night, wondering what it all means.

I had to stop and ponder myself when they kept repeating the phrase "How am I not myself?" How am I *not* myself? How am I not *myself?*

Truly, how could I NOT be myself? By definition I am me. I am myself. A tautology. How could I not be me?

Nevertheless, we tend to disown parts of ourselves at a deep level. I dare not be myself totally. I cannot be me exactly as I am. There are parts that are unacceptable, and other parts where we feel lacking.

The disowning begins when we are told that who we are is not enough or is not good enough. It begins when we are told that we are too much one way and not enough another way. That happens repeatedly, over and over in our lives — in subtle ways, and ways not so subtle.

Our response is to seek to be someone else, someone who we are not. A person who would be more acceptable in society, would be more liked by our family and friends and would be more liked by ourselves.

Perhaps we respond by hiding parts of ourselves or by attempting to change certain of our traits. By not being ourselves totally, we attempt to be more acceptable and liked. By trying to be different, we aim to please. We try to become someone else.

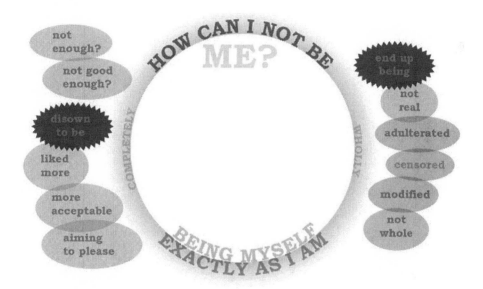

That "someone else" certainly is not the real me, because the real me is all polarities: stupid and smart, loud and shy, harsh and gentle. That "someone else" hides those qualities that are not acceptable to me and those around me. Perhaps it is because I was too loud in a situation that called for quietness. When I disowned my loudness, I also lost it for the situations in which I need to be loud.

When I cease to be loud in any situation, then I have disowned a part of myself. That distorts who I really am because I only have one half of the polarity. The disowned parts make me fractured, not whole. I cease to be me being me. I am modified, censored, adulterated, and not the whole real me.

The question remains: How can I *not* be *me*?

When we try not to be ourselves, we run into big trouble.

When I was a child, there was a time when I wanted to find someone else to be!

One by one, I considered the life of each of my friends, thinking what it would be like to be each of them and to have their life. I did not see any imperfections in them when I looked at first. I thought others were more perfect and had a better life than mine.

This most likely was coming from a place of not wanting to be me, because I felt inadequate. I felt that there was something wrong with me.

I did not see anything wrong with my friends, so I thought that being one of them might be a way out. That might be a way to be adequate, be right with myself, if only I was someone else. I looked very carefully, and I actually went through considering each and every friend and their life.

I was surprised! I saw imperfections and flaws that were not apparent at first in the first friend that I considered. Then I looked at another friend, because again, on the surface, she appeared perfect, with perfect parents and a perfect life.

Again I saw that her life was not perfect, and she showed me some things that I did not want to have in my life. Then again, I looked at another friend, and was surprised to find the same thing.

I came to the conclusion that they were not perfect and they did not have a better life than mine. I eventually realized that they were each flawed in a different way than I was. I would not trade my life, as imperfect as I thought it was, for their lives when I saw the imperfection in them as well!

Then I decided it was just as good to be myself, because I was not more or less flawed than they were. There was no advantage to switching who I was because all the other possibilities were not perfect either.

In addition, I would never be able to be them anyway – let's be realistic. No matter how much I would have wanted to trade my life for my friend's if I found it better than mine, there was no way to actually do it.

Therefore, being myself is the best — and turns out to be the only — option. I accepted who I was to some degree in that decision.

Being myself means not censoring any part of me, as well as not falsely exaggerating any part of me. It is being me, just as I am, that's all. No more; no less.

Being me as myself is just fine. Warts and all. Beauty and all. Being me as myself is loving all parts of me. It is letting all aspects be there, with no judgment. The letting be without judging takes no effort at all when I am resting in this present moment.

I experience being myself as me resting in myself. That takes no effort and no struggle.

The struggle was trying not to be me! What a relief to simply be me with no struggle and no effort, and simply rest in that. What a wonderful feeling! What a wonderful life!

I saw that there is no use trying to be anything else. Besides not being possible, it takes effort to try to be something else. I've been through that.

You've been through that. It's time to stop the trying, stop the effort, and give ourselves a break. We deserve this kind of break today. Letting go of expectations and simply resting in being ourselves, we can be who we really are.

Being YOURSELF is the primary and a comprehensive principle in this Golden Universe. The implications are huge.

Resting in myself, I realize I am resting in mySELF, the broadest and deepest definition of who I am. I am resting in my immortal SELF, my omniscient SELF, my omnipotent SELF, the part of me that is everything and is outside of time and space.

Resting in mySELF gives me everything, and the less effort I put out, the more easily everything I need comes to me. This is extremely satisfying and fulfilling.

Simply resting in who I am brings enjoyment to life. There is lots of joy in feeling satisfied and fulfilled. In addition, it is easy!

There is joy in who I am when I am resting. There is joy in this present moment as I am resting here. There is joy filling the whole Golden Universe resting in this present moment.

You may think it is easier said than done. Anyone willing to give up effort and drop the societal expectations and live true to who they really are will find it is worth making that choice.

That choice of being me, only me, is the same choice as to rest in this present moment. See how clever that is? See how simple that is? Resting in this present moment gives me the Golden Universe. Resting now in this present moment gives me myself exactly as I am. The Golden Universe has requested of me and given me permission to be only and precisely who I am. That way, I can play the exact role the Golden Universe has picked out only for me.

Now life is an adventure of discovery and unlimited exploration. I have discovered so much by resting here in this eternal moment. I have explored a lot, and I have so much I am curious to explore. The exploration happens right here, right now, in this infinite Now.

It is a relief to simply be myself. I don't have to think about it or do work to bring in disowned parts of myself. I simply rest in this present moment, letting it show me who I am. I let this eternal moment present to me avenues of exploration.

I go on the adventure of a lifetime, simply by resting in this infinite Now!

2.3

Principle 2: Follow the lead of Nature

In exploring life in this Golden Universe, our adventure is within Nature. We can see the way the Golden Universe operates by observing Nature. We are part of Nature and the way we work is not apart from her, even if we try to be separate and superior.

By divorcing ourselves from nature, as if we actually could, we create something which is not the Golden Universe. The only place we can be separate from Nature is in our minds. Thinking we are separate from Nature is unnatural, and it leads to suffering in the long run.

That mental separation is not the reality of the Golden Universe. Therefore, the workings of Nature will always prevail, because we are made up of nothing else but Nature. In a baseball analogy, Mother Nature always bats last.

The way we work will always follow Nature; we cannot truly be separate from her. Therefore, it is wise to study natural processes and follow the lead of Nature. We can learn a lot by resting in Nature and taking her lead.

Nature has cycles, and balances herself in those cycles. We can too. Day follows night and activity follows rest. Both are necessary.

Too much of one or too much of the other will not feel good. You will know when it is time for rest after activity when you listen well. You will know when it is time for activity after rest when you are paying attention.

For me, I can hardly do anything else but move when I have rested enough. My legs get restless and I get an image of a hiking trail or my city streets. Off I go!

In addition, I can do nothing but rest when I am done with being active. My body longs to be horizontal at times. It leads me to a chair to sink into. I know for sure that it is time to rest then. At the end of the day, I wind down and know it is time to go to bed. My bed is calling me to rest.

Day-and-night cycles are broken down and repeated in smaller cycles and smaller cycles, down to the minute or second. Therefore, not only is it productive to rest at night, but also periodically throughout the day.

Taking breaks from a concentrated activity or flow of activities creates refreshment when activity is resumed. I know this by paying attention to the energy in my body and mind. You also know when you need to take a break — and when the break is over.

There are seasonal breaks too. Winter is a long rest, and time for nourishing seeds. On the other hand, summer is activity and the flowering of those seeds.

We participate in different activities in the winter naturally, because Nature has dictated it due to temperature or weather or length of the day. Summer invites us to be outside in the warm air and get active. By following the lead of Nature, we can maximize the enjoyment of every time of year.

If you feel like going inward in the winter, go ahead and read more books, spend time baking or cooking warm foods in the kitchen, write in journals, do inner work. Spend time in quiet conversations with loved ones. This can nurture the seeds of the new growth that comes with the change of seasons.

By being at home with what Nature is offering, we can move with her cycles. Winter to spring to summer to fall. Sunrise to morning to high noon to mid-afternoon to evening to night. Sitting down to do work, to getting up for a break, to working some more, to changing it up by playing and so on.

The Bible verse from Ecclesiastes echoes in my head: "To everything there is a season, and a time to every purpose under the heaven."

There is a purpose for each season. Each offers a different experience which complements and balances and flows into the others. When we are flowing in these cycles of Nature, we are balanced by being in harmony with the different experience of that season.

In the same way, moments of the day each have their purpose. There is a time to eat and a time to do chores. There is a time to spend with family and friends and time to spend by myself. There is a time to focus and be active and a time to relax and rest.

Resting in this eternal moment shows me how to flow with the time of day. That is how we live in the Golden Universe. Noticing everything that is contributing to and is present in this moment is a great way to be at home with what I am doing at this moment.

I notice a body signal of hunger. It is not a thought, but an actual signal from my body. I go and eat. I feel that hunger satisfied through another body signal.

When Homer Simpson hears the word "donut" or sees something in the shape of a donut, he pictures a donut and is hungry for a donut. That is not a body signal. It is a thought arising from past programming. Distinguishing between what is presented by the Golden Universe and what is programmed thought helps us flow through life in its cycles.

Being at home in the purpose of each time of day, in each season, I recognize an appreciation for the activity in which I am engaged.

2.4

Nature becomes more in complexity

By appreciating "What Is," what is here in this present moment, Nature expands and gives us more. All creatures in creation appreciate and give back to Nature. We give to each other, and in so doing, make both of us more.

All of Nature is always expanding in becoming more. One way it is evident is on the physical level. In the natural process of appreciating and becoming more, Nature becomes more complex and integrated.

It is not enough for Nature to just have more quantity of herself. What would we do with more and more single-celled organisms? Nature wants more quality.

What Nature does is turn in on herself and revisit what has been created, then add a new layer or dimension of complexity. The way Nature becomes more complex is by integrating what has come before with new ideas, combining them in a complex, novel way.

Those cycles of Nature are not just going around and around in circles! Nature's cycles are moving in the three dimensions of space and the fourth of time (and more!) and we can see them as tracing a spiral. Each time around the cycle, more is added. The spiral shows new layers or new dimensions. There may be a fifth dimension and a sixth dimension, and so on, if only we open our awareness to notice.

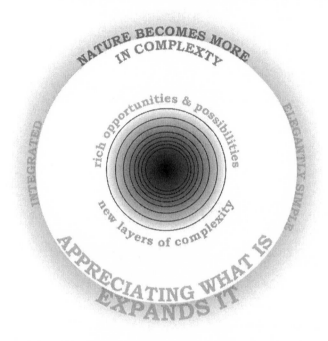

We don't have to study the science of it and have a mental understanding of it to notice! We can notice it in our daily lives, in nature around us and in us. More complexity is being created. That results in richness and more opportunities and possibilities for everyone.

Due to the elegance of this process, more complexity does not lead to more complication and confusion, because the complexity is integrated.

The Golden Universe expanding and becoming more complex happens in an integrated way. This "more" of the Golden Universe, including and building on what is already here, is elegantly simple, making sense. In turn, the new integration opens to even more new possibilities.

Nothing is really outdated in the Golden Universe, because it becomes new when another layer of the spiral is added in an integrated way. Everything is used and useful because it can have a different purpose in a different context.

That swells my appreciation even more and more, because unlimited potential is in my hands. It is the nature of how we are living. It is a natural process.

Examples are everywhere in nature. One of my favorites is how cells started to become more complex by integrating a bacterium as an energy-producing organelle inside them.

There was a bacterium that was efficient at producing energy. It was at a dead-end in itself because it was about as complex as it could get as a bacterium. However, there was an opportunity with other cells that wanted to grow more and become more complex.

These evolving cells integrated those energy-producing bacteria inside them, and it became a win-win situation. The production of energy was specialized in an organelle, now called the mitochondria, which came from integrating bacteria which did just that.

This integration allowed cells to grow more and specialize more, creating more-complex organisms. We as humans owe a lot to this integration, because every one of our cells has these energy-producing organelles, the mitochondria, which came from bacteria.

Like the story of the bacteria and simple cell integration leading to more complexity, and even human beings, appreciation leads to even more expanded experiences. In those experiences, there is another principle at work in this Golden Universe.

It is a principle that, perhaps in missing it, in its apparent absence, you can notice and realize when it was there before. It is something you perhaps don't see every day.

However, when you do recognize and realize it, you start to see it everywhere, all around, all the time.

Principle 3: Miracles

This third principle of the Golden Universe is noticing miracles. I did not say working miracles, but noticing them. Miracles are happening all the time. When we tune in, we can notice them.

Things that seem to happen miraculously are called miracles because we don't see how they happened. We don't understand the workings that caused them to happen. Nevertheless, how they happened is also within the laws of Nature and the purview of the Golden Universe.

Miracles take place during perfect resting in this eternal moment.

In resting here, we can notice clearly the abundance all around us. We can notice the source of all giving rise to what is surrounding us. We can appreciate the infinite wisdom behind what is happening, even if we don't see it at the moment. We can appreciate the all-knowing, all-present, benevolent aspect of what is happening all around us.

Just knowing that miracles happen, and resting in that place where they happen makes sense of all other principles.

It makes sense of being ourselves. It makes sense of living in the cycles of nature. It makes sense of the integral spiral of creation. (Or is it fractal? Both seem accurate descriptions!) These unseen principles are always working in our favor, so why not call them miracles?

When someone calls just when you need to talk to them, is that a miracle? When the means to pay for something you need shows up, is that a miracle? How about flipping the switch and light flooding a darkened room? How about when a flower blooms?

If we don't know how any of this happens, why not call it a miracle?

The flower is following Nature's principles. Most of us would consider it to be a miracle because we do not see how blooming happens and we ourselves cannot make it happen. It's simply the flower's unfolding according to its Nature.

We may never know how to experience the way the bud forms, then slowly opens to bloom into a flower. It is responding to forces it feels keenly. The beauty of the flower and its unfoldment speaks of a miracle.

In the same way, when we grow and transform, is that a miracle? When we transform from our experiences, it is from resting in this present moment. Here, we rest knowing that all is well with the transition from one thing to another.

In order to grow, we need to let go of old forms, just as the bud needs to be released, then open into the flower. Our changes are beautiful while in process, and they create more and more beauty in the world.

We don't necessarily see how releasing the old forms leads to something greater. We don't necessarily feel that it is beautiful when it is happening. A caterpillar does not see what being in the chrysalis is producing, but a butterfly does appear. Looking back on the transformation, I would call that a miracle.

When the world seems to make the least sense, remember that there is a more integrated, more beautiful, more compassionate world being created out of the seeming chaos.

We can't see the next level of integration from this one. It may look disjointed and may feel cruel. But from the biggest messes are created the most beautiful ideas and structures.

Look into your own heart to see the truth there.

2.6

Everything that comes to us

We are given desire by the Golden Universe.

Desire flows through us in order to fulfill our particular individual piece of the Golden Universe. We fulfill our mission as the Golden Universe by following these desires.

These desires are pure when they arise and come directly from the Golden Universe. It is possible to corrupt that desire if we taint it with the programs of the past and the motives of the little self.

When desire flows pure, it comes direct from the Stillness, powerful and unstoppable. It comes to us automatically and our eyes are open to all possibilities. When our eyes are open to the heart of the Golden Universe, we know the purity of these desires.

When we see through the stillness and peace of the Golden Universe, the desires coming to us are the desires of the Golden Universe. They are always coming to us, whether we notice them consciously or not.

We are always surrounded by the Golden Universe's perfection, whether we notice it or not. These desires are how that perfection plays out.

By accepting the Golden Universe's desire for us, we accept things the way they are. When we go with what is coming to us, we are in the Golden Universe's perfection.

When we are living in this perfection, it is so easy, so natural, so joyful that there is no desire to ever live any other way. The desires twisted by past programming are seen for what they are and lose their attraction. The choice to follow the desires of the Golden Universe is easy when we see everything that comes to us from following them.

It is easy to turn away from a twisted desire when we are able to distinguish the pure desire underneath from which it originated. Following the desires of the Golden Universe, we see that no matter what a pure desire may lead to, the Golden Universe's desires are bringing the best for us.

Everything that comes to us is the Golden Universe's desire for us. If that looks like loss, then it letting go is necessary in order to make room for a more expansive good. If that looks like an unfortunate turn of events, then watch and give it more time for the Golden Universe's goal to become more apparent.

We may not want to go through loss, or people seemingly turning against us, but these are some of the ways the Golden Universe can arrange it so that the best comes to us. It is not all loss and pain — most certainly not.

The Golden Universe brings us the best in the form of joy and love and beauty. When our eyes are open to the gifts of the Golden Universe, then we see how it brings us everything for our fulfillment.

2.7

Desire is the source

The Golden Universe's desire for us is to rest in this moment.

Desire draws us here because it is the place of most contentment, most fulfillment, and most joy. Everything in this present moment is here to serve.

Everything done from this present moment is service to us and all around us. When we are resting in Now, just now resting, we are devoid of the past with its programs and twisted trajectories for us.

When resting purely in the Infinite Now, creation is in this moment, only this present moment. Therefore, there is no past available to taint it. There is no future anxiety to twist the creation in this present moment. There is nothing of the small self in creation in this moment. What we do while resting in this eternal moment is devoid of a personal agenda.

Everything that comes to us from resting in this present moment, and living only from here, is our highest desire. Therefore, what flows through us serves all of creation. What flows through us in terms of action is grounded in the highest good for all involved, so it is pure service to each other.

It serves the highest purpose and desires of the one resting now, and being moved to action, and it serves the highest in those surrounding, rippling out to the whole world.

The river of desire of the material world, the manifest world where we live and breathe, surges upward. Desires serve in leading us to fulfill our purpose in the Golden Universe. Desires are given by the Omniscient to guide us through this physical world.

If we did not have a desire to eat, we would waste away. If we did not have a desire for community, we would not do things for each other, so we would not thrive. Desires are the way that we interface with our highest purpose.

By being driven by our bigger purpose, step-by-step desires become evident in this manifest world.

We are led by our desires to produce the fruit of our action. We play in this world to fulfill these desires. That is the only thing that is satisfying. That is the only thing that propels us upward to the next step and the next step and the next for our growth. We are fueled by our desires — and that leads us to where we must go, where we are destined to go, where it is in our nature to go.

Our mundane, manifest desires are a stepped-down version of our highest desire. They function to get us through to the bigger picture of our highest desire. We never know where we might be going, although we might have a general idea. We mostly can see where our desires are leading us in the meantime.

We can always be inspired by our desires, because they are a coming from and leading to a deep well of wisdom, purpose, and contentment in this life. We feel the deep wisdom in the desire because it gives us contentment both to fulfill it and in the process of fulfilling it.

Desires are both the vehicle and the journey.

We never know where our desires will lead us. That encourages us to be innocent with those desires. When innocent, we accept them for what they are, not projecting to where they might lead. The one thing we can be sure of is that they are always leading to our highest desire when resting in the eternal Now.

When we follow desires from resting in this present moment, they always lead us to more. More fulfillment, more action, more love, more beauty. More is the way of the infinite.

When the infinite is brought into this manifest world, it fulfills its identity also by becoming more; in that way that there is more complexity and more integration. There is more love embodied, and we more easily can be perfectly, precisely ourselves.

The more in this world comes from desires shot like Cupid's arrow into our hearts by the Golden Universe. The Golden Universe sees the big picture, so it can trigger the desire in just the right person at just the right time in order to orchestrate a wonderful, purposeful happening. What happens is always for the greater good of all.

When we participate in what is happening, we may not know our role in the big picture. However, when we are true to our desire, when we give to following that desire 100%, then we are able to participate in life fully. We get to live our own life fully.

Boundaries between "me" and "the world" dissolve so that we can appreciate the fullness of the Golden Universe. We realize that we *are* the Golden Universe. We get to enjoy the fullness of us as the Golden Universe here, Now.

As we perceive a desire of the Golden Universe while resting in This Present Moment, the fulfillment of that desire is automatically present. The rivers of desire and fulfillment run together in this present moment.

The river of desire flows through us to make us unstoppable. The desires flowing upward are magnificent. They are blessings in this world. They pull in the resources of this world as well as the un-manifest world in order to make the most of this experience. They connect to all others playing with desires in the same way.

Desires never contradict each other when playing this way. They always build something complex and beautiful for all to see.

The twin rivers of desire and fulfilment are at home in creativity. They flow through our lives for the benefit of all. We create our lives following our desires and we create the world fulfilling those desires in this Present Moment.

2.8

Resting in this Golden Universe

What we are here for?

What is our purpose in this Golden Universe? Do you have any idea?

Or are you disillusioned and think that there is no purpose?

Our purpose in this Golden Universe can be looked at in many ways. The simplest is that our purpose is to be ourselves, completely. That brings us back to the first principle: Be Yourself. Completely, without reserve, be who you are.

In order to be ourselves completely, we must know who we are. Not "who we are" as in our name and job and whether we are outgoing or introverted. We must know who we really, really are, underneath our individuality. Specifically, we can know who we are as seen by this Golden Universe.

The Golden Universe sees us as nothing other than itself. It contains us and we contain the Golden Universe. Boundaries dissolve, and we are the Golden Universe — we are nothing other than ourselves, one and the same.

The Golden Universe appreciates that we are in bodies. We are the body of the Golden Universe.

Through us, the Golden Universe can express itself and interact with itself. This is the way it can know itself more. It does that because we know ourselves more.

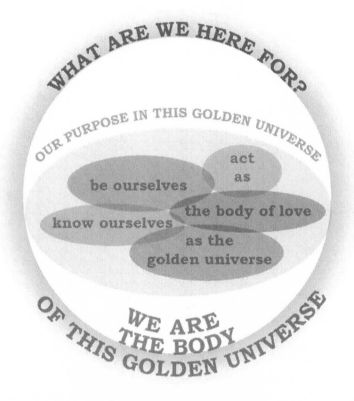

And the Golden Universe knows itself as love. Since the Golden Universe knows itself as love and *is* love — and we are the Golden Universe in actuality — we are the condensation of love in bodies. We are the body of love. We are love in action.

What that means is h-u-g-e, and has so many implications and ramifications — so many that it can take all of life to experience.

One consequence of being love is that we can't do anything wrong. Nothing at all is wrong or out of place. Nothing ever was wrong with us.

That may be a startling statement. You may not agree. What do you mean I can't do anything wrong? If I hurt someone, then I am doing something wrong, no?

You tell me that there is nothing wrong in the world, with all the miserable people and miserable conditions? Somebody or a whole collection of somebodies is not doing anything wrong to create this misery?

I'm saying that there is nothing wrong from the point of view of love. Love embraces all, allows all, includes all. Love finds a way. Love finds a way for more love to manifest. It finds a way for love to spread and make love conscious to those not conscious of it.

It follows, then, that everything that happens, happens to enable more love to come to us.

Every experience is taking us to a greater experience of love. Everything is happening to make love more conscious. When it seems that it is happening in a roundabout way, be sure that it certainly IS happening.

When it looks as though the worst has happened, we can rest in the knowing and assurance that it happened that way so that we can experience more love.

In those situations, I suspend judgment, knowing that I do not have the whole story. On occasion, I have even said to myself, "God works in mysterious ways."

Most often, the rest of the story is yet to be revealed. I cannot see it because the rest of the story has not happened yet, or I have not seen its implications. The rest of the story will show me the gifts of expanded love in what just happened.

For example, I was traveling to a conference in Niagara, Canada. My trip involved flying to Buffalo, New York, then taking a shuttle service to cross the border, then to a hotel in Canada.

I was waiting at the airport in Buffalo for the shuttle service. When it arrived, I tried to follow the driver to the shuttle. However, I thought I was going somewhere different than where the shuttle was. I got lost in the parking lot, and went around in circles. I did not find the driver, so I returned inside the airport to wait for the next shuttle.

As you can imagine, I was upset. Maybe in my situation, you would do what I did. I started berating myself for the confusion and the delay. I blamed myself for missing the shuttle and wasting time. (You see, I was still in that mode of valuing efficiency!) That was one time I did not suspend judgment.

However, love prevailed.

While I was waiting for the next shuttle, some other participants in the conference arrived at the airport to wait for the shuttle. One was someone I had met and talked with at other conferences.

We chatted to pass the time, and I found out that she had booked a room by herself, as I had. Therefore, we decided to share a room when we got to the hotel. That worked out the best for both of us, both socially and financially — and it would not have happened if I had not been delayed for my shuttle departure!

When I was sitting berating myself, waiting for the next shuttle, I did not know the rest of the story. It was easy to be negative and blaming from that perspective. However, soon enough, the gift showed itself!

2.9

The hand of the Creator

In following the desires coming from the Golden Universe, we facilitate the direction of creation. We serve as a hand of the Creator in this Golden Universe to develop ideas and see them come to manifestation in the world.

We are an instrument of creation, and we are positioned at the cutting edge of creation. Isn't that exciting?

All of us resting in this eternal moment become the instrument of creation in this Golden Universe. We are then able to create the fullest Golden Universe possible.

Creation is happening, we are part of Creation, AND we have a hand in creating.

That is where our utmost responsibility is to act as the Golden Universe, to act for the good of all, to act without a personal agenda. Responsibility is "response ability" as we are able to respond creatively to what comes to our attention.

We act as the hand of the Creator in the Golden Universe by first observing what comes into our awareness, to our attention. Then we engage what is presented to us by acting. The action comes of itself when our attention is resting in this eternal moment, and the actor, us, is identified as one and the same as the Golden Universe.

There is no one who knows better how to act to increase our own joy and freedom than we ourselves do, as we follow our deepest desires.

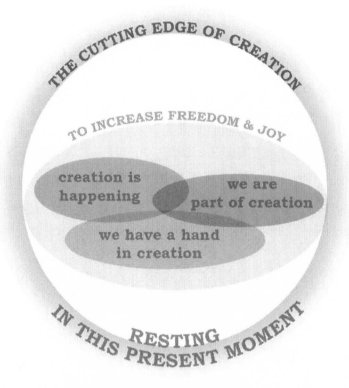

However, when action happens from the perspective of resting in this eternal moment, it goes way beyond personal joy and freedom. Done from this eternal perspective of Now, the action is for the freedom and joy of everyone and everything.

Advancing our own happiness and love allows the same to grow in this Golden Universe.

That is exactly how more and more ideas and inventions for ease of living are created in this world. We are the instrument of that happening. We take delight in seeing new things and furthering creation, because the Golden Universe takes delight in these same things.

Furthermore, when effortlessly resting in this eternal moment, we know how to best tune that instrument, which is the body, to its purpose.

Remember, that purpose is the same as the purpose of the Golden Universe. It is important to keep our instrument finely tuned, because we are the hand of creation in the Universe — and the more finely we resonate with the creative principle, the more joy and fulfillment we experience in our lives.

The fine-tuning of this instrument happens when we rest in this present moment.

Being the hand of the Creator in creation happens from this present moment, Now.

Knowing the biggest context possible, dreaming the biggest dream, happens from this present moment. Resting here, now, is the key to being the cutting edge of creation.

If you think that in our lifetimes, more than any other time in history, the greatest harm is coming to society and the Earth — look again. I'll bet that each and every generation thought that over and over again.

When we cannot see the direction of the big picture, we may think that the destruction or dismantling of something is a disaster. The old ways are no longer followed. The structure that thrived not so long ago is crumbling. Without the big picture, it looks like a downward spiral.

Instead, what is happening gives way for the new to be built.

The new includes and transcends what preceded it. Therefore, it looks chaotic as the pieces are being re-assembled. This most certainly is happening now. It has always happened, and we recognize it happening with increasing speed now.

When we see that this is the way, we see that the destruction or dismantling of what came before takes place in order to restructure now. When we accept the fact that it happens for more expansive creation, then we can more easily let it go.

In letting go, we can take in what is happening with joy. We can take a bigger perspective, even if we don't yet see how the pieces are coming together.

All we have to do is play our part in what happens. We do what we are inspired to do. We let what is happening happen, and look for the greater thing being created.

As you survey creation from the perspective of the Golden Universe, it is easy to feel joy and appreciate beauty. It is everywhere.

Appreciation is a matter of choice as to how we look at what is here. Certainly, something beautiful can be found when we look for it. Then we can appreciate it. Joy expands with appreciation.

When we see what appears to be destruction, it is the same. We can see the joy in what is passing away, and we can appreciate the ability to surrender to the new and see the beauty of it.

It never is a waste. The pieces of the past are integrated into a new perspective, and become more. They become more useful, more joyful, more an embodiment of love.

This is a call from the Golden Universe for us to get on board with this. Appreciating everything expands beauty and joy in the world for everyone. To rest in this eternal present shows us the way forward.

How great is creation like that!

III.
Living in flow
in the infinite now

3.1

My life started flowing

> *All there is to be known can be known by intuition. By mastery of intuition, the perfection of all other practices is had. Just as when you befriend the emperor, all the empire desires to serve you, just so, all the perfected aspects of consciousness bow to one who has perfect intuition.*
>
> — MSI

There was a time in my life when I first noticed overall that things just seem to flow. It was not that I had periods of being in the flow; it was that all my life was in a flow. It is possible you may have noticed this too.

The change in my life was hard to describe at first. The experience was that things just happened with ease, and the best things came very simply and naturally. I was not thinking about making things happen. I was not aware of what was the best to happen; it just came to me.

171

At that point in my life, I was starting to consistently live by what is called intuition. I did not label it intuition at first, because the sense of what was happening was subtle. It was just beyond comprehension, and I did not have the big picture, but there was a sense that things were happening differently.

Things happened almost like miracles. I did not see how things were happening. I did notice they were all happening for me, for my greatest benefit.

When I tried to describe it to someone else, I was uncertain at first what it was, but then I recognized that the term "flowing" applies. Yes, one action flows into the next and I show up in just the place it appears I need to be. There is the next thing, then the next and the next.

There is no sense of doubt; there is no interruption of the flow. It just keeps happening. One moment seems to bleed into the next. Yet it is always this moment — but it appears to be changing from one scene to the next.

When your experience is like this, you can be sure that you are living by intuition. When you live by intuition, life keeps growing in depth and breadth.

It is helpful to recognize that flowing is not just going and going and going like the Energizer bunny. Flow is not at a constant pace. At times, flow slows down and goes around the bend. Then it may speed up again. Other times, there is a slowing down almost to stopping.

Ebb and flow — the flow of life goes back and forth like the waves at the beach. Flow gently comes and goes in a predictably unpredictable rhythm. It is steady in continuously flowing, but the speed and pace varies.

We can rest in the whole experience of flow. As we can't control it, can't push it, can't slow it down, all there is to do is rest in the flow.

When flow is ebbing, there is an opportunity for restorative rest. It is not a time to push the river of flow. It is not possible to push the river. Full forward flow happens again on its own, and pulls back again on its own. This is a natural rhythm. The ebbing is a gentle pulling back, but it never actually stops.

Perhaps that is what we fear the most: that when the energy is pulling back, it will stop and never flow forward again. The ebb pulls back and decreases in speed at an ever-slower rate, until the movement is almost imperceptible.

Then there is the point of inflection where the movement changes direction and flows out again.

While doing Tai Chi, I feel this same ebb and flow in my body as one movement leads to the next. I sense going from fullness to emptiness and back to fullness again. Movement is slow, then slower, then even slower: then it changes direction, then moves again, slowly at first.

My arms are lifted up, in slow motion, then almost completely stop at the zenith. They change direction as sinking happens as my knees bend and arms descend. My core turns, turning my knee and foot, and my arms follow along until everything has gone as far as it can and then pulls back again.

Ward off, roll back, press, on and on and on the body flows in one direction, slows to the point of inflection, then moves in the next direction.

That kinesthetic sense applies to life as a whole for me. I am in the flow, going with the flow, letting the flow move me, flowing through life.

Go with the flow

The concept of "going with the flow" can carry some distortions and misconceptions with it.

Being in Flow is the most masterful way to be, according to the way I define it. However, the idea of "going with the flow" can be used irresponsibly and as an excuse for not meeting commitments.

"Oh, I did not make it to the meeting because I was going with the flow." It can be used as a frivolous reason to do what I want based on past programming or habit, explained as choosing to "go with the flow."

Also, someone who doesn't care may say they are "going with the flow." It may be the path of least resistance. You see, that "path of least resistance" can be unconscious behavior, or in the flow. It can be careless or carefree. It takes attention to, and familiarity with, the deepest meaning of flow in order to "go" with it.

Flow is not carelessness. Instead, it allows us to be carefree. When we're going with the flow, all the cares in the world are being taken care of by the intelligence of where flow originates. That frees us to not have to manage it, not have to control, but instead to relax into the intelligence of flow.

In other words, flow is not a superficial thing about doing what everyone else around us wants us to do. It is inner-directed, with openness to what is being presented at this moment. When our attention seizes what is being presented to us in this moment, we make the most of opportunities and can go with the flow.

We can be aware of all the potential in this moment when resting in the eternity of Now.

Doing that, we can be aware of choice, which is also being moved from within, from Now. I may have a notion, an intention, of what I want in this moment, how I want a situation to turn out, and I surrender it to the flow as well.

I experience going with the flow to be a combination of awareness of what is being presented, awareness of my inner being and what serves it, and allowing whatever is happening to happen from the perspective that it is all happening for my growth and to know who I truly am.

Allowing whatever happens to happen is not our usual pattern. We have a tendency to want to control things for a certain outcome. We almost always have an agenda. Allowing is something we can master when we see its benefits.

Allowing means to not fight against what is happening in this moment, or what has happened in the past. In fact, what has happened in the past can have no impact on us now when we allow everything. We may be in a situation that is the consequences of what happened in the past, but that does not mean there has to be any suffering. Each situation in which we find ourselves can be fresh and new.

We can make of it what we wish. It is up to us, and us alone. What we do now has consequences, for certain. To

178 | Antidote to Overwhelm

be guided by resting in this present moment in what we choose to do will make it the most enjoyable life.

What is being presented now is not under our control. Allowing reinforces that idea. We are not in control about what happens or has happened in the past. Our response to allow is the only control we have in the situation.

What we choose to do now is where we have control. We can act out of our previous programs, or follow inspiration, to act for growth. In acting out of our programming, we are not in the allowing space, because habits control our actions.

By the way, following inspiration is the act of most enjoyment. We can always allow inspiration to come through. That is part of allowing.

When we come to the point that there is nothing to do but allow, life becomes easy and enjoyable. It is supremely enjoyable because there is no blame as to what has happened in the past; there is no shame about what has happened in the past. It is as if the past does not exist.

When there is nothing to do but allow, things happen as if by themselves.

How easy is that? There is no sense of a "me" doing things, yet they happen right in front of this person I call "me," with "me" as the instrument.

More amazingly, things are happening for me outside of my conscious awareness, as if things are being arranged behind the scenes. I benefit from the things that happen and I see the benefit when I see what has happened take center stage.

By resting in this present moment and going with the flow, we are surrendering a "personal will" to a greater will and purpose.

When we do that, there are no dilemmas, there is no debating, there is no suffering a decision. The decision has already been made. We simply have to act it out.

It is not hard to rest in Now and let things happen. It makes things so simple and easy and enjoyable!

3.3

Flow is enjoyable

I experience Flow as supremely enjoyable.

What does enjoyable mean? What makes something enjoyable? Simply, what is joy?

I find that people think that we have to be "over-joyed" in order to experience joy.

"Over-joyed" is over-the-top, excessive, party-like exuberance, and jumping up and down. I picture sports fans' reaction when their team has won the championship. Joy in excess is also the over-excitement of a child on the night before Christmas. This kind of joy is exhausting because it is imbalanced. It is joy taken beyond its healthy limit.

However, I see people who think this is the only manifestation of joy. They think this is what joy has to look like to be joy.

Jumping for joy is one aspect of joy — and then there is enjoying. Simply enjoying. This word connotes a more balanced, even experience, and yet it is still an experience full of joy.

Life is supremely enjoyable in every moment, in every activity, when we allow and go with the flow. I experience and know this. Going with the flow is letting life live me.

To enjoy life, I don't have to be jumping up and down. In fact, I feel joy as a kind of self-satisfaction, contentment and fulfillment as I am enjoying a moment, every moment. I rest in and enjoy this eternal moment.

There are times when I do get excited with joy. There are crescendos and decrescendos of joy in my experience. Nevertheless, I detect a baseline of enjoyment and fulfillment all the time. My life is joyful. I enjoy life.

Enjoyment comes from being in this present moment and allowing the life force of the Creator to direct the play. By allowing in this present moment, I don't know what is coming to me and for me. That gives the element of surprise. It allows life to bring me delights that are something I couldn't even imagine. That is enjoyable.

Being playful is ultimately enjoyable. Play has an element of surprise as well, because we don't know what will happen when we do something new or different in a playful move.

Play is the interactions of various combinations of the fruits of manifestation and how they play off each other. Peach-mango. Banana-orange. Blueberry- cranberry. Mmmmm. Delicious play of flavors off each other.

Life is like that with people too.

People can come together in play and produce a wonderful, creative product. That is what innovative businesses do: create products that improve the quality of our lives. That is what community groups do when they have an event for celebration, like a Fourth of July picnic and fireworks. It is enjoyable to meet new people, create something new, and be surprised by the creations.

An artistic person can play with color, texture and shape and produce a wonderful, creative product, which we call art.

We can play in nature by simply appreciating and enjoying nature. That is called living in enjoyment, or joy, if you like. Remember, it doesn't have to be bungee-jumping or some extreme sport. Sitting quietly or walking along appreciating nature is enjoyable.

Joy is part of the fabric of the universe. If you still yourself enough, or when coming upon a beautiful scene, you may catch the Golden Universe in effulgent joy. It may surprise you and cause you to catch your breath.

In fact, this happens only if and when you resonate with the Golden Universe yourself. Only if your energy is finely tuned in that moment does the effulgence of joy shine on you. It shines in you. In reality, you are catching the effulgent joy of yourself, revealing your own true nature.

You are resting in joy, simply and beautifully, by being totally present in this eternal moment.

3.4

Flow is easy

People object to things being easy because they think things don't work that way. "Easy will never get you the good things in life," they say.

Easy connotes laziness. Easy implies that there is less worth, because maybe you didn't work hard for it. Easy can also mean that there is no challenge, or not a worthy challenge. When something is too easy, then there is less value.

Easy rarely means that whatever happens, happens because you are in the flow; you are in the zone.

Nevertheless, that is what easy means to me. Things can be easy when there is a "me" out of the way and things are simply happening. That kind of easy is supremely enjoyable.

When we are in the flow is when things happen with ease. Perhaps using the word "ease" instead of "easy" is more palatable. I want my life to flow with ease. That sounds better than wanting an easy life.

An easy life connotes not having challenges; and without challenges, there is no growth, a fundamental human need. But to meet the challenges with ease sounds completely enjoyable, because it connotes growth as well as the sense of looseness and relaxation around it. Ease signifies the opposite of stress.

Oh, did I use the word "stress?"

Stress is in our cultural awareness, a buzzword for everything that is making our lives hard. Stress is what shortens our lives. Stress is what makes life miserable.

Good stress is what nudges us to grow and become more. Bad stress is what kills us. Stress is inevitable in this day and age. Stress is inescapable in our culture. It is easy to be stressed!

Bad stress is not even in the picture in a life with ease. Yes, there are challenges which call forth growth, and they are not experienced as what we know as "stress."

The antidote to stress is to define challenges in this present moment. Things can be challenging in order to encourage us to grow. These challenges can look huge in our lives. However, resting in this eternal moment, we get a perspective on those challenges.

Resting in this eternal moment, we can only pay attention to what is being presented in this moment. It is impossible to be overwhelmed in this Now.

We take life in, bite by bite, what is presented to us in this moment. Actually, it is even more fluid than taking bites. Perhaps a better metaphor is drinking in what is before us. Experiences flow like a creamy milkshake (or being politically correct, a green smoothie) flowing down our throat.

We drink in life as we rest now in this present moment. Nothing can get caught in our throat. Nothing makes us choke. Resting now, all happens easily and effortlessly.

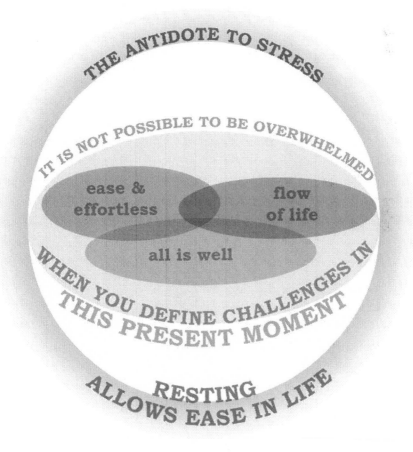

This ease and effortlessness is the flow of life. With flow, there is no doing, so there is rest. With flow, the best is happening, so we can rest back and enjoy.

While things are flowing, we may notice a sense of resting more and more. There is no need to control. There is no need to manipulate. There is no need to project into the future with worry. There simply is a sense of resting.

Resting in Now, resting in who we are, we are resting in the sense that there is nothing to do — yet things get done. We are resting in the sense that everything is attended to in its time. The sense is that we will know when to do something, because it will happen of itself, in a sense.

The sense is that we don't have to meticulously plan what to say or do. Easily and effortlessly, from this perspective of this eternal moment, what we say or do comes out of our hearts.

We can prepare for a speech by designing the flow of the speech ahead of time, so that when it is time to give the speech we can rest in this eternal moment while the message is delivered. We do not have to memorize a speech, but we can do things to ensure its easy flow when the time comes. Having the message in our hearts, we can rest and give the speech from this eternal moment.

Resting is fundamental to how we live flowing through life. Resting allows ease in life.

Consciousness resting in itself is the source of all manifestation. Awareness resting in itself is the source of all individualization. All beings resting in their being makes the world the place it is.

No matter what is going on in the world, all is well. No matter what is going on in our lives, from this sense of resting, we experience that all is well. Resting in the sense that all is well, we have a different perception.

Have you ever been somewhere new and the colors and shapes and textures seemed so vibrant and alive? That is perception from innocence.

When we can wake up in the same place every day and have this perception of the vibrant aliveness of our surroundings as well as our inner being, then we know we are resting in the innocent awareness of our being. We are living with ease.

Seeing vibrant, alive colors and scenery fills me with appreciation of beauty and love of life. I am easily resting in the innocent awareness of my being.

Smelling the unique smell of the air in this moment, in this season, and catching a breeze fills me with elation. That is resting in my being, simply resting in innocence.

Feeling the breeze on my skin or the sun warming me through my clothes brings me a centered aliveness, leading to the feeling of celebration. That is resting in the awareness of who I really am.

While resting, hearing the deafening Silence — while the sounds of the world around filter through — brings elation to me. Tasting color and smelling sound and hearing beauty is a sure sign of resting in the awareness of expanded being. Our aliveness can seem hyper-alive with exalted experiences sometimes. That is exciting, but it is not a necessity nor is it a goal.

Resting in the stillness of the source of being, while watching my body performs some actions, makes life simple. Everything happens from resting, and there is no need to be conflicted about decisions. That makes things simple and easy.

Just as you might suspect, when you rest in the awareness of your being, you have made things as simple and easy as possible.

This simplicity and ease is the hallmark of resting. How much effort does it take to rest? How simple is it to just rest?

Giving up the idea of having to do the right thing, having to be a certain way and having to follow society's rules, makes things easy and simple. You can fit in with society and "do the right thing" from the inside out, so there is no effort and no conflict.

I recommend making things as easy and simple as possible.

3.5

The skill to go with the flow

Going with the flow is resting in our pure, true nature. It is not resting in who we think we are.

Who are we really? What is our pure, true nature?

We have become accustomed to identifying with the collection of thoughts that run through our head. These thoughts are who we think we are, not our true nature.

These thoughts running through our head tell us that we are good in math but bad in sports. Perhaps they tell us that we are pretty or handsome or not, or that we are not good at business.

These thoughts tell us "ten thousand things." None of what they tell us is relevant to who we really are.

> *"The nameless is the beginning of heaven and earth.*
> *The named is the mother of ten thousand things."*
> — Lao Tzu, *Tao Te Ching*

The more we identify with these thoughts, the more that we think this is who we are, the more limited we become. When we believe that our thighs are too big or we will never rise in business to become a boss, then we are identifying with thoughts that we believe are true for us and as a result limit us.

The way to get beyond the limits of those thoughts is to rest in this eternal moment.

From this moment come actions which are not limited by those thoughts. As long as we don't pick up the belief in the thought, we are free from it, naturally. There is no process to go through, no procedure to follow. The only thing to do is rest in this present, eternal moment. When we do that, we rest in our true nature.

Our true nature is unlimited, although at this moment we may not be boss material. We are in essence unlimited, even though we are not good at tennis. The potential is here and can be developed by skills if desired. Skills can be developed by intentional practice, but desire is necessary to actually apply yourself to practice. It turns out that practice is more important than talent. That does not mean that anyone will be as good as Serena Williams at tennis. She was given talent, but more importantly, she has the insane desire to develop her skills to the extreme.

One person may be more adept at a specific skill because of their makeup and their previous experiences, but we all can develop skills with proper guidance. The question then becomes whether we want to develop a specific skill.

Once it is certain that we want to develop a skill, then desire is the key to whether we will be able to master that skill. Most of us can become skillful at basic things.

Those skills we have a desire to pursue are the ones our soul is asking us to develop for our fulfillment.

When we are able to put 100% into mastering one skill, then it is sure to be mastered.

It is our desire that fuels the 100% attention to this skill. That desire has to be here first. Then a 100% commitment makes it more certain that we will master this skill.

A funny thing happens when we do this. When we put 100% into mastering something, then other parts of our life start to fall into place. We become more skillful in other aspects of our life, just because we are mastering this one skill.

Therefore, why not start with the skill of resting in this present, eternal moment?

Resting here, now, gives flow in life. We can return to resting here, now, whenever we notice that we have picked up a thought or feeling instead of letting it flow through. We can return to the flow of life. It becomes a skill to rest here now, to be in the flow.

As we practice this skill, it becomes apparent that it is our natural state.

In fact, the naturalness of this state of flow draws us back into the flow when we have sharpened our skills. The skill fulfills its use then, because it has made itself obsolete. We develop the skill of resting in this eternal moment; then this moment becomes so attractive that we don't want to be anywhere else. No skill is required at that point.

When learning to flow through life, there is nothing else to do but flow. If we have momentarily flowed over the bank and left the central flow, the bank gently nudges us back. Developing this skill brings this kind of return.

Developing the skill of remembering to rest in this present moment not only gives us this eternal moment; it also enables other skills to develop naturally.

Flow has no attachment to outcome

If you are a sports fan with a favorite team, then you know what it is like to have a desired outcome.

We root for our team and feel pain if they are behind in the game. We feel loss, grief and depression when they lose. Our desired outcome is a win for our team, and we hold on tightly to that.

We groan when they make a mistake on the field; we cheer when they do things well. When well-designed-and-executed plays result in a score, we may jump up and down, whooping and shouting. Our whole body is involved in the outcome. Our mental and emotional state is dependent on the outcome. We may have a bad day when they lose, a good one when they win.

That is the definition of suffering!

Being dependent on outside circumstances sets us up for unpleasant consequences. It is a thin line that separates winning from losing.

By only being happy when our team wins, we set ourselves up for failure. Sure, the UConn women's basketball team, the Huskies, had a 100-plus-game winning streak, including two national championships. They can expect to win again. That is very rare. How is your favorite team doing?

In the same way as we love our favorite sports team to win, we can get attached to the outcome of actions or intentions in our lives.

That sets us up not only for suffering, but also for missing the gift in whatever happens. Suffering happens when what we want to happen is not what is happening in front of us, and we don't accept it. That misses the gift in what actually *is* happening. The gift of what happens is only and ever in this eternal moment. As we rest in this present moment, the best of life is coming to us, no matter what it looks like.

If we are determined that things go a certain way, that we have our way in life situations, then we exclude a bigger creation that could happen that is beyond our imagination at the moment. That bigger creation is available by resting in this Infinite Now.

Being attached to the outcome is being determined to operate out of our thinking mind, and not allowing the omniscient Creator to play. All power, all knowledge, all creativity is in play in this eternal moment. We miss that when we are attached to outcome.

Face the facts: The bigger creation from the Infinite is always in play anyway. We don't have control over the outcome.

When we have the illusion that we have control, we are mistaken. Sometimes that leads to a rude awakening and suffering.

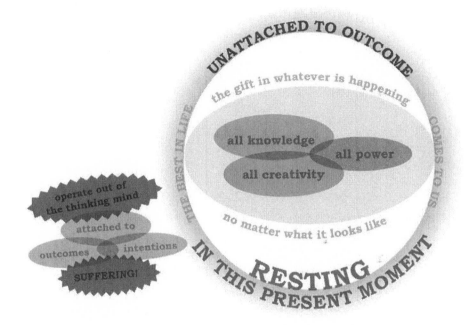

Suffering is not necessary, because there is no suffering when we are not attached to the outcome. The way we can be sure we are not attached to the outcome is to rest in the flow of this present moment.

When I was visiting Hawaii, I loved to see as much as I could in the time I had available. However, I put myself in the hands of my host on the "Big Island" to get us places and help choose what we wanted to do.

After visiting the top of the active volcano Mauna Loa, we decided to see where the lava from the more active Kilauea enters the ocean. That involved parking in a designated area and hiking what my host estimated as two miles each way to the viewpoint. We started in the early evening, so we anticipated hiking in the dark.

However, after we got on the trail, the first sign we saw said "3.5 Miles to Viewpoint." That meant the hike was four miles each way, a total of eight miles! My host expressed that he might not want to do that. I was not quite sure I wanted to do that either. My daily walks are two miles.

As this was a once-in-a-lifetime opportunity, I did want to see the lava hit the ocean. That's why we started this trek.

However, as I was resting in this eternal moment, I said with completely honesty, "I am happy to be hiking, and am not attached to getting there, to the viewpoint." He agreed, so we kept walking.

I was aware that at any moment he could decide to change direction and go back. As I truly was not attached to the outcome, I was okay with that. We kept walking. And we kept walking while it got dark. And we walked some more.

Finally, we made it to the viewpoint. I was not attached to this outcome. However, it was satisfying and joyous to make it there. We could witness land being formed from the lava flowing into the ocean! I took some pictures and rested.

We still had four miles to walk to get back, and I reminded myself to not be attached to that outcome as well.

As I was getting tired and my feet hurt on the way back, it took paying attention and choosing to not listen to the thoughts about how far was left to go. I was resting in this present moment, walking, and that was all there was to it. I was enjoying every minute of that walk back by resting in this eternal moment.

When we saw the outhouses at the two mile mark, I was happy to see them as I rested back in this present eternal moment. I kept playing with the experience of eternity being now and eternity being the time it took to get back to the car!

Resting in this eternal moment won out. I was not attached to getting back to the car either. That made the walk back enjoyable. I enjoyed the changing view of the rising moon, the clouds on the horizon and the lava under my feet.

3.7

Flow is paying attention inward

Being aware Now and paying attention to what is coming in from our senses, we can be filled with sensations.

We may first notice the gentle breeze on our face, then the smell of coffee brewing. Next, we notice the taste of the first sip of coffee. Meanwhile, the sound of birds chirping in the morning fills our awareness. We see the sight of the sunrise.

In addition, we may sense what the body is doing: breathing, the heart beating and skeletal muscles tensing and relaxing.

By filling our awareness with these sensations, we risk putting all our attention outward. We can miss the inner focus of resting in this eternal present moment.

That which is inside is watching; there is an observation point inside, which is aware of the sights, sounds, smells, tastes. It is possible to be aware of Now first, before letting the sensations float through our awareness.

The first step of not putting all our attention on the outside world is to be aware of what is coming from the senses from that inner observation point. As long as we watch those sensations and don't completely identify with them, the observer is at work.

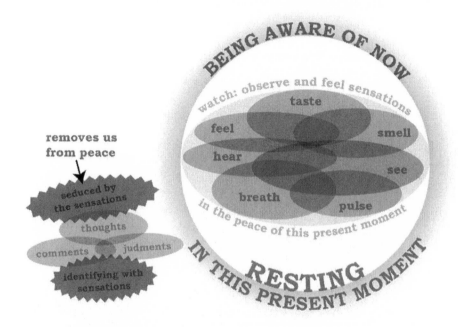

Not totally identifying with the senses means we can observe as well as still feel sensations. For example, we can feel the throbbing of a stubbed toe, but we can be watching it from a perspective of the observer where our decisions are independent of the throbbing sensation.

The observer viewpoint gently notes what is going on without making a value judgment of good or bad, win or lose.

Without that context of watching, the throbbing toe sensation can take over and can lead to self-defeating thoughts. Before we know it, we have concluded that this is a bad day. Then the next thing we know, we have dripped toothpaste on our shirt. The day starts snowballing while one thing after another happens, making us miserable.

When we watch these sensations from a still mind, we don't have to identify with the sensations. In fact, these sensations pale in comparison to the stillness of the mind. This is what I observe.

When I go to the dentist, the assistants marvel that I don't want anesthetic for the drilling. They claim it hurts them so much that they can't do without it when they get their teeth drilled.

My experience is that drilling my tooth feels like pressure and vibration. Those are sensations I can observe. Those sensations are not life-threatening, nor are they unpleasant. They are simply sensations of the body that I observe.

In observing them, I am not labeling them as anything more than what they are: sensations.

In observing the sensations purely in this Infinite Now, my mind does not go off on thoughts like "When will it be over?" and "If it feels like this now, what happens if it turns to pain?" There is no thought attached to the sensation. It is simply a sensation I observe in this present moment.

The sensation is nothing in the context of the fullness of this present moment.

In the rare case when it seemed like the sensation was overwhelming my attention, I can still rest back and watch it. It is possible to have a broader perspective even in that situation.

Because I have a habit of watching and not identifying with these sensations, I can apply watching to this even stronger situation. At first, I needed a tool, a technique to shift my attention back to watching. Anything can be watched when you make a habit of it.

The habit starts with a choice. We have a choice as to where we put our attention. We may choose to watch the sensation, along with the thoughts generated by it.

Most likely it is difficult at first to purely watch the sensation, since there are many thoughts, comments and judgments about the sensation.

For example, a stubbed toe can throb, but when we think "I'm clumsy," or "Why does this always happen to me?" these are comments spawned from the sensation. In addition, further judgments like "I will always be clumsy and therefore never be popular at school" perpetuate a downward spiral.

It is by watching thoughts and making distance from them that we can prevent downward spirals and in fact find peace. It is by drawing our attention inward that we avoid being seduced by sensations and miss the peace of this present moment.

In the peace of attention on this eternal moment, we can be involved with upward-spiraling emotions and creative projects. In this present moment, we can find healing on all levels: body, mind and spirit.

The flow of healing in the body

What is the first thing an old-fashioned doctor says to you when you are sick?

Rest.

We may think that more rest does not apply to us, that we are superhuman and can keep going. Or we may strongly believe that if we don't keep going, all will fall apart.

That is a strong belief I see at work in a lot of people who come to me who are sick. It seems to be epidemic in our society: We must do more, do more, and do even more.

That is part of the pathology; that is why we are sick.

Doing more does not necessarily equate to enjoying life more or having more to enjoy in life. It seems like it would, or we would not be doing more.

If having to do more is coming out of a sense of survival, then that is misguided as well. The more we do to survive, the more we have to do to survive. What we focus on grows. Therefore, if there is not enough for survival, and we have to do more to survive, there is no end to the more we have to do to survive. Therefore, we will just barely miss getting beyond survival over and over again.

The pattern keeps repeating because we are focused on what we don't have – which is the means to survive. To turn that around, it is necessary to switch focus to what we do have and are here to do. Then we keep growing that.

Then surviving will turn to thriving and doing takes care of itself.

The pressure of having to do more, for whatever reason, leads to imbalance and sickness. It can be sickness of the emotions, mind and body. It truly is sickness of the spirit.

In order to heal sickness, on whatever levels it manifests, we need to stop doing what makes us sick. We need to stop in our tracks. We need to rest.

Healing, the true restoration of wholeness, demands rest. Restoration, "rest-oration," has the word "rest" in it. Healing demands the rest of our body, the rest of our mind and the rest of our spirit. After all, isn't it overdoing things that time and time again gets us into trouble? Whether we think it is necessary to rest or not does not matter; it still is overdoing it that got us into trouble.

The antidote to overdoing it is simple. It is as simple as resting in this eternal moment.

Doing that, we see how simple it is. In this Now, this Infinite Now, there is all doing and all not-doing. There is all potential and the realization of all potential. There is thriving and full enjoyment of life.

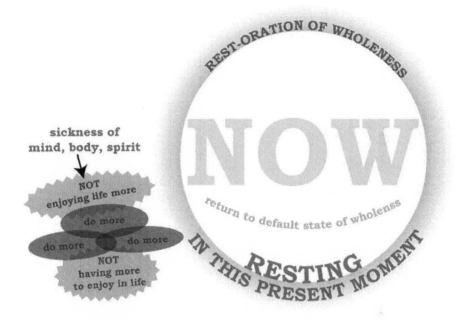

By resting here, now, we unleash the power of getting things done without having to do more and more. By resting in this Infinite Now, we see things get done from this Now, not from our self that is focused on survival and having to do more.

Resting in this eternal moment, there is wholeness — there is healing.

Resting Now is most powerful because it allows everything to return to its default state of wholeness and health. Resting now shows us that fundamentally, we are whole.

We always have been whole, always will be whole, and most certainly in this present moment, we are healed and whole.

Resting here is powerful healing. We hardly know exactly how powerful it is.

3.9

Healing from resting in this present moment

One summer evening, I was hiking down a mountain trail to a swimming hole with a waterfall. My friend led the way as we wound down the limestone gravel trail. It led beside the Glorietta River, which springs from the top of a mountain, its cold water cascading down, pooling in areas for us to enjoy on a hot summer evening.

While hiking, I am always careful with my footing, picking my route for the most stable place to land and step down again. At one moment on this hike I suddenly found myself on the ground on my butt. I didn't see it coming. I had no hint that something was unsteady or about to happen. I simply found myself in an instant sitting on the ground.

As I was resting in this eternal moment while hiking, what transpired was a bit different from other slips I have experienced on the trail. Before, I would blame myself and be a bit embarrassed that I had fallen, and get up as quickly as possible.

This time, I sat there and continued to rest in this Infinite Now.

It was a surprise that I had slipped, and the moment continued to unfold from that point with complete curiosity and innocence. Time seemed to slow down.

Initially, I noticed what was presented to my senses. First I noticed that the palm of my left hand was aching. Looking at it, I noticed that the palm was starting to swell and I could see a little blood under the surface of the skin and muscle.

Then I noticed my right hand, which was holding my precious camera. It was still palm up, clutching the camera safely, but two knuckles were scraped and bleeding and getting my attention. Finally, what came to my awareness was that my butt hurt on the right side where I was sitting on the dirt between two rocks.

I followed my first inclination and cleaned the scrape on my knuckles with some saliva, tasting a bit of grit. I watched the wound, and it was bleeding very little.

Not rushing, I next decided to take off my backpack. I took it off arm by arm, and then got up.

At that moment, I wished I had packed homeopathic Arnica, as it is the perfect remedy for trauma and bruising. Then I remembered that I don't have to have the actual tube of pellets to get the effect of the Arnica. My companion and I sent the intention of homeopathic Arnica to me and my injuries.

Then we continued down the path to the swimming hole.

The bonus of this pool was that it is cold mountain water. What is better to reduce the swelling of an injury than cold water?

When I say cold, this pool was reeeee-ally cold, chilled in its underground source. However, when I submerged completely, my body generated heat to warm me. It was amazing, feeling the cold water on my skin and the heat radiating from my core!

Perhaps this held another benefit of resting completely in this present moment.

I did not project ahead to be fearful of the coldness of the water. I did not remember other times I had plunged into cold water and felt uncomfortable. I did not expect to be cold from the cold water. I simply, innocently, curiously dove into the water and rested in this present moment to watch the experience.

Yes, I sensed cold water, and it was simply an experience I felt in the Now, not something to avoid.

It is amazing how quickly my body responded with radiation of heat from my core. My companion experienced the same thing.

I also purposely rested on some rocks, sitting in the water with my butt and hands completely submerged, noticing the coolness on the swollen areas. If I was at home, I may have done the same thing with cold packs.

Then I swam around and enjoyed the waterfall.

The hike was not at all marred by this occurrence, because I was resting in this eternal moment and I let whatever happened happen.

Healing possibilities were presented to me, and I never interpreted the sensations at the injuries as pain. It was simply that those body parts were telling me that they were affected and wanted some attention, and it was no big deal for them either.

The body knows how to heal an injury. With calm equanimity, I proceeded on the hike and through the completely enjoyable evening.

One day later, another element of healing showed up.

I was a bit sore that next day, partly from the longer-than-usual hike, and partly from the bruised body parts. By the way, the swelling was actually minimal, and there was very little discoloration from the blood in the bruise on my palm.

A bit more than twenty-four hours later, when I was relaxed and meditating, lying on my back with my feet up, the most astounding aspect of the healing occurred.

While meditating, which is a profound way to rest in this eternal moment, I noticed a free-fall feeling. Next, my whole body jerked, starting from the point of impact of the fall the previous evening. It was just one movement, as if I was shaking something off, then deep relaxation again.

It was a surprise, since I expected nothing but relaxation while meditating.

I had heard of this sort of thing before, but I'd never experienced it in such a clear, direct way. That whole-body jerk was a release of the impact of the fall! It was the final healing element to release the physical concussion of my body.

First, while meditating, there was an obvious momentary falling sensation. However, I did not land, defying gravity's inevitability. There was no hitting the ground!

Instead my body moved in the opposite direction, jerking up, releasing the kinetic energy that it had absorbed previously. It was an un-doing of the impact of that slip and fall on the mountain trail. It was happening to me in such a clear and profound way that I just had to include it as an example here.

There is nothing that happens while resting in this Infinite Now that is not for greater awareness of who we are and our potential in life. Healing happens in this present moment, and we may not even know what is being healed.

With this most pointed example, there was a clear awareness of what was being healed. Nevertheless, it may have carried with it healing of previous falls — and injuries and who knows what else.

For me, it goes to show that every moment resting in what is, resting in this eternal moment, there is the fullness of life.

In that fullness, things can happen that look like unfortunate events, but when experienced from this moment are simply part of what is happening. There was not any need to make sense of it.

In the days after the fall, and while healing from the fall, I was able to have a wider perspective. At first I dismissed it — then it dawned on me what the significance of it was. Now, I appreciate the experience even more.

What a profound experience of healing from this Eternal moment!

3.10

Rest and let the Healing Power of Nature do its magic

Whenever we are injured or getting sick, we tend to slow down automatically and can't help but rest. In fact, slowing down may be the first sign that something is off. Miraculously, sometimes resting will do the healing by itself.

When we rest, we let the Healing Power of Nature do its magic. A lot happens for healing which is below our conscious awareness when we are resting.

The Healing Power of Nature is evident when a scratch or a cut heals without our conscious attention. However, the Healing Power of Nature goes so far beyond that.

Health is our blueprint. Nature is always working towards fulfilling that blueprint whenever and however possible. Nature is the architect and the builder.

When we remove obstacles to the manifestation of the blueprint, Nature, knowing that blueprint, will rebuild according to it.

Most of the obstacles to the manifestation of our health are from the thoughts we hold in our awareness and the beliefs from which we operate. When we rest in this eternal moment, our cells have the opportunity to return to their default state of health.

When we sleep at night, this exact process is going on. Our cells begin to eliminate waste products and renew themselves. Unfortunately, we usually have done more damage than can be restored in a night.

By continuously resting in this Eternal moment, we allow the Healing Power of Nature to restore our cells. By having no obstacles to each cell manifesting in its clearest purpose for our health, they are allowed to return to more optimal functioning.

When each cell is functioning optimally, we have vibrant health.

Each cell has the ability to function optimally, each cell has the desire to function optimally and each cell will function optimally unless we have given it a directive to do otherwise. These directives come from our own beliefs and thoughts. They come from old, entrenched programs.

Fortunately, none of those programs, thoughts and beliefs is operating while resting 100% in this eternal moment. While resting here, Now, all our cells have the opportunity to return to their most optimal functioning and health.

I have seen people appear younger, the longer they meditate and practice resting in this present moment. Not only is their appearance younger, I would bet their cells are younger and more optimally functioning.

The Healing Power of Nature is certainly at work while resting in this Eternal moment.

Intuition is living in the flow of Now

Who knows what is best for you?

By resting in this present moment, you will know. Especially if you don't impose "shoulds" and social norms on it, you will know.

What is beyond the thinking mind, below our programming, that insight will come through when resting in this eternal moment. When we rest in Now, we get direction from what is known as intuition.

You can't judge an action as coming from intuition or not, just by what the action looks like. Actions are known by the consciousness of the one who acts. The only one you can play this game with is yourself. You cannot accurately say whether something came from intuition purely from what the act is.

Were you resting in this present moment, then the action just came? Or were you unconscious with lots of chatter

220 | Antidote to Overwhelm

in your mind? No matter what was going on, you could have been speaking or doing all varieties of activity, but was the action coming from resting in this present moment?

If yes, then it was from intuition. If no, it was a knee-jerk reaction from the programs by which you have been living. That is the distinction.

It is possible to cultivate your access to inner knowing, which can lead to living by clear intuition.

One way is to use an imagination exercise. I learned it from my friend Ellen Solart. It involves your feelings as well, again, those feelings beyond emotion, but emotion can do while you cultivate this. This exercise goes like this.

When you have to make a decision, try on each possibility.

In your imagination, see, feel and put yourself in that particular situation in as much detail as you can flesh out. As you are sitting in that possibility, then look inside and feel how it would be to have the possibility happen.

If you feel joy and gratitude, then you know it is the one for you. If you feel contraction and discomfort, then keep trying on and tweaking the possibilities until you find one with joy and gratitude.

For example, I have used this in a restaurant when choosing which menu item to order.

I know that not all chicken is created equal, and the waiter's opinion of the best dishes may not suit my taste.

So, if chicken sounds good, I'll read the description and let the feeling of it resonate while resting in this present moment. If it brings me joy and satisfaction, then I go with it. If not, I keep looking.

As you play with this exercise, it may happen that new possibilities open up that are a slight tweak to the situation — or they may be whole new options. You will find one eventually that feels joyful and fills you with gratitude.

This is the one that your intuition is leading you to!

In my restaurant menu example, I may like the chicken dish if only it didn't have the side of tomato and peppers. I may ask for potatoes instead. If the chef can make the substitution, then I feel joy in all aspects of the meal.

Or the waiter may recommend something similar, which lights me up — like barbecued pork with potatoes — and that may instead match my desire resting in this present moment.

It may take practice in order for intuition to come clearly. It can be very playful and fun.

As intuition is our inner knowing, it should not be a stranger. Don't let concepts and beliefs about whether you can be intuitive stand in your way. We all have intuition operating, whether we have taken advantage of its workings or not.

Most importantly, when you are playing with this, do not hang onto what happened in the past. Do not let the past color whether or how your intuition comes through.

Play innocently. The intuition coming through is innocent, so simply match it. Don't take it seriously, whatever you do.

When you get the hang of living by intuition, remember that you can always grow in using it. Intuition will guide you to take the next step, both in your use of intuition and in what is next for you.

Let go of the past, and having to remember everything. Let go of what happened and how it affected you. Let go — and let intuition guide you innocently in great adventure.

Once intuition is on board, you are well on your way to finding and remaining in joy and happiness.

Clear intuition is a result of resting in this eternal moment and letting all its gifts come our way.

Intuition and Skills

The other side of developing intuition is developing skills.

We had to gain lots of skills as children in order to learn how to live in this world. We started with the motor skill of nursing and grasping. We progressed to sitting up, crawling, standing, walking, and eventually moved to riding a bike and driving a car. We learned a multitude of social skills and cognitive skills in school, within our families and with our friends.

Skills pertain to our navigating through the manifest world in many ways. Besides the physical coordination for many tasks as well as social skills, we gained skills in how we relate to our mind and spirit.

The skills on the earth plane are the most obvious. Too often, we judge ourselves for not having a skill that would seem to be a basic life skill. Perhaps we do not get along with certain people well. Or we don't know how to prepare food. Whatever our skill set, we all grew up needing different strategies to get along. All skills have their uses.

The world goes around by the butcher trading his skill for the plumber trading his skill for the bus driver trading his skill for all the jobs there are in the world.

In addition, this world values highly those with exceptionally well-developed skills. Professional athletes, doctors, lawyers and CEOs get paid well for their expertise.

Cultivating skills is what keeps us growing and maturing, and keeps us feeling alive.

In fact, the development of skills is something essential to growth. Not only is growth fulfilling, it is also a natural part of the expansion of our awareness while resting Now.

As we develop mastery in one thing, we have the opportunity to keep increasing the level of challenge to match the skills we have developed. When we do so, we rest in this present moment, acting in what is called the flow state.

The work of Mihaly Csikszentmihalyi is focused on studying people in the flow state. This state is one of complete enjoyment of, and immersion in, this present moment — a state in which we feel totally alive. He describes my experience perfectly.

He shows us that the flow state is only possible where the challenge is high and where there are skills to meet it.

In other words, we naturally experience the flow state when we are using our athletic training in athletic performance, such as scaling a rock face; or using our facilitation skill in running a meeting smoothly and productively; or using creative skills in designing a building, or for a musical or other artistic endeavor. We are in the flow state in these and so many more moments of life, when we are completely letting the action happen through us with the skills we have developed.

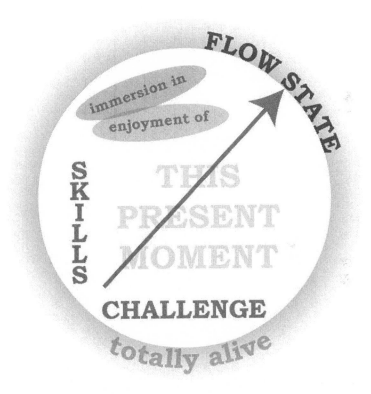

Dr. Csikszentmihalyi says that when our skills become developed, we must up the challenge or we fall out of the flow state.

I have found that there is more than one way to up the challenge. One is by increasing the difficulty of the challenge, and the other is by increasing the attention focused on the task at hand.

For example, I have been washing dishes since I was a kid. I have developed skills to do that efficiently and effectively. I can intentionally challenge myself in some way, or simply rest fully here in this eternal moment while I wash dishes.

While washing dishes, I could make the challenge to wash as an expressive dance with music playing in the background. I could wash by acting out the rhythm and pitch and excitement of the music. I could respond to what is being presented to me as a musical background in this present moment.

Someone else might want the challenge of getting everything clean in the shortest amount of time. That would be an enjoyable challenge if it was playful and not forced.

Life is about doing the dishes, or having someone else do the dishes for me; life is about the ordinary things in life. Why not make the ordinary extraordinary? That is our potential in life, to make every moment extraordinarily enjoyable.

In fact, it is our inalienable right to be able to enjoy every single moment. It may simply require a shift of attention, a shift of perspective to make this possible. Every moment counts. There are no gaps in life that are the hiccups between times of enjoyment. Life can be a continuous party of enjoyment.

To make it simple, I rest more deeply in this moment while doing things that seem ordinary. I rest back, and rest again, and rest some more to have all my attention in this eternal moment. When I do have all my attention on this present moment, I rest back and watch the dishes getting cleaned by my own hands. There is no effort, and there is no boredom.

If my attention has strayed, I may notice thoughts like, "Boy that is a lot of dishes," or "I should have done these yesterday so that I wouldn't have so many today." Those thoughts come only when my attention has strayed from this present moment.

Washing dishes in this eternal moment has clarity and aliveness and ease and enjoyment, as does every experience in this eternal moment.

Doing things we consider ordinary is an opportunity to see each moment as fresh and new, and to let life flow. That brings enjoyment to the ordinary to make it extraordinary.

3.13

Resting in intuition

Most often, I experience intuition coming through as action before thought.

Woah! Does that sound dangerous to you? Isn't that what we have been warned against, to not do anything without thinking about it first?

Stay with me, and I will bring out the finer points of what I am experiencing.

Intuition comes from resting completely in this eternal moment. While resting here, I am not thinking. I get a clear knowing to do something. In fact, I may be doing it before it registers by the mind what I am doing. The mind may want to chime in after the fact and explain why I should do it, but I am already doing it.

It may be speaking without planning what to say. It may be turning left onto the road before I knew that was the way to go to get where I wanted. It may be choosing to buy something, then finding out later why I needed it.

Intuition can come into play both for big decisions and for small, everyday choices. It is operating every moment, so take advantage!

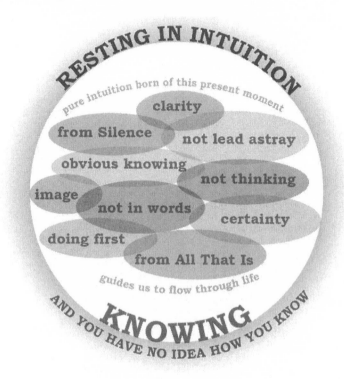

Before going on a long vacation, I packed an extra hair tie. There was no reason I could think of to do so, because I had other barrettes, but I felt compelled to pack the second one. As it happened, I lost one hair tie on the first day I arrived. Of course, I could have bought more while on vacation, but that problem was already solved when I packed two hair ties. I even said that to myself when I discovered the first hair tie missing: "So that's why I packed two!"

In any case, intuition comes from a silent place rather than a reaction. Intuition comes from resting here Now.

Intuition is important to cultivate, because it shows the way which is the best, not only for you, but for everyone around you — and for the whole world.

When we all live in the world through our intuition, then imagine what we can create! I am flowing through my life and you are flowing through your life and our lives are flowing together in the matrix of flow which is the world.

On the personal level, intuition brings us the most happiness. More importantly, following intuition makes every step of the journey happy.

Intuition is not just a woman's faculty. It is used by all the great scientists, writers, artists, and creators in all arenas. All great inventions involved an intuitive insight, and we get these daily too.

Intuition is simply the part of us that is in intimate touch with all that is, and so can bring to our limited perspective something that otherwise would be out of our imagination. Every problem is solved at a level beyond that in which it is perceived.

Every day of living can be lived by intuition. It will not lead us down blind alleys or lead us astray. Too bad we think there is a mind that wants to be in control. That is what leads us astray.

The next time you are faced with a choice, practice intuition. If you can catch yourself before the logical mind starts grinding on what are the advantages and disadvantages of each side, you can be still and become aware of what your intuition is telling you.

It will be an obvious knowing.

Do not look for lofty words from an angel or your "higher self." Most likely it will not be in words. However, if you do hear words, examine carefully if the knowing came first or the words came first.

Intuition may come in a flash of an image. That's how I create visual art.

I see the next line or shape in the flash of an image, then make the artwork in front of me look like that. Subsequently, I get the next flash, and on and on. Bit by bit the artwork takes form. I also get a definite knowing when the piece is done. When there are no more flashes, there is nothing left to do; the art piece is done.

Intuition may simply be a knowing that you have no idea how you know, but you have certainty about it.

I remember one time consciously playing with this.

I was being very still and watching my mind. I knew I wanted to go and talk to a certain person who was in the neighborhood where I was staying, not far away. This was a time before we all had cell phones.

As she was a busy person, I didn't want to interrupt her. I also did not want to spend time going to look for her. In addition, I did not want to have a lot of other people around so that I would have to wait to ask her about the issue.

As I sat there watching my mind, I realized that I could strategize when she was most likely to be there, and also not surrounded with too many people. Unfortunately, there would be no end to trying to figure it out! I would only know if I guessed right when I arrived there. It is interesting that I put so many conditions on this meeting!

When I finally let go of all that and forgot about it, I continued to be still and watch my mind and meditate. Suddenly, there was one moment when I got up and started over to where she lived. I recognized that the getting up was not preceded by a thought to get up. I simply observed my body getting up. That was just a little startling, but also oh so informative.

I could act without thinking about it beforehand! That was pure intuition.

When I arrived to talk to this busy person, she was there and the conditions were favorable to talk with her and take care of the issue. That little exercise reinforced for me that I was doing — acting through intuition — more often than I realized. I became more comfortable with letting go and letting intuition come through.

Let your intuition take the lead. You don't have to feed it anything other than your attention. That's all it needs. Rest in this eternal moment — and let intuition take the wheel.

It is only pure intuition, born of this present moment that easily leads us to flow through life.

Intuition presents with a knowing, which is evidence enough. I notice that the mind likes to chime in and explain the knowingness. However, it always happens after the fact of the knowing that appeared in my consciousness first.

Intuition's knowingness is primary.

3.14

Resting erases doubt, drops confusion

You may find yourself in a situation in which you are full of doubt and confusion.

What is real? Is this my intuition?

It is so confusing. I can't make any sense of it. I feel one way in one moment, then another in another moment. How do I decide?

Doubt and confusion are the efforts of the mind to cloud clear knowing and maintain control. It is the habit of the mind to want to control things, and it is not possible for the mind to control when resting in this eternal moment.

Slipping out of eternity and back to into the mind, I notice that everything seems confused. There is a mixture of feelings and thoughts and they seem to make sense for a while. Then confusion reigns again.

Doubt is a product of the mind. The mind can never be satisfied enough to eliminate doubt. Doubt manifests as a thought that we tend to see as an evaluation of what is happening. "I doubt that I should do that after all, because I don't have the time, money, or energy." "I doubt that he knows what he is talking about and I won't listen to him. But then, to whom should I listen?" We doubt when we believe those thoughts running through our mind. We will always have doubt if we rely on the mind to give us answers.

The only thing that erases doubt is resting in this present moment.

The mind is meant to be a servant and not the master that so many of us have made it. As a servant, the mind can process input, but it is not a good guide to how things are going. It will steer us wrong and give an inaccurate picture of what is happening.

This is because the mind's function is to produce thoughts, and thoughts by their nature are judgments.

Consider this simple example. When we think that something is blue, we have judged that it is not any other color of the rainbow. Physicists will tell us that the thing is absorbing every color but blue, and reflecting the wavelength of blue, which our eyes see. Right there, we know that it is not absorbing blue, but we judge it to *be* blue, since that is what we see.

That judgment is an interesting fact about something – it is blue. At some point, thinking it is blue can be a limitation, because it is a judgment. What does it look like after dusk? What does it look like under a red light?

This simplistic example becomes much more personal and complex when it comes to judgments about us and the world.

However, it shows the workings of the mind. If we cannot even be sure if something is blue, we must have doubt about everything else in our experience. This doubt comes from taking judgments from the mind as useful and valid information about our experience.

We cannot rely on the mind as a source of information about our experience. It is the servant for processing the information coming in from our senses, both physical and subtle.

We have a habit of letting the mind lead. It takes a simple skill to retrain to let the mind be the servant. By not allowing the mind to lead, we can put the mind in its place as servant and allow it to function. Simple tools and techniques can help immensely in loosening the mind's grip on our attention. By using a tool to go beyond the mind, we can retrain ourselves.

That retraining skill also involves making distance from our thoughts and watching them as if they were on a movie screen. When making that distance, we can realize that we are not our thoughts as we watch them. They are going on independent of us.

Thoughts keep flowing, one into the other, flowing through the mind. Thoughts have nothing to do with us, although we may have believed before that they do. We are not our thoughts, even though that is where we have gotten our identity.

Watching thoughts, we may see them arise independent of us and lead to another thought. One thought leads to another, then another, and possibly disappears, to be replaced with another seemingly random thought. We call that stream of consciousness — but it is actually stream of thoughts.

Streams of thought are not consciousness, because consciousness is what the thoughts flow through. Consciousness is the container of the thoughts. Consciousness is our awareness, and it is who we are.

If we can notice something, it is something arising in consciousness, since we are the background awareness itself. What we notice is what is flowing through our consciousness.

What we don't notice is what we end up retaining as our identity. There most likely are thoughts that we did not see arise when we were watching the mind. Those thoughts sound like "us." They have our voice.

Those thoughts we still retain as valid information about us.

Those thoughts are the ones that cause the deepest doubts because they tell us that we will never amount to anything. They tell us that it is okay to not do what we really want to do. There is a wide variety of thoughts that we cannot see, and therefore we take as our identity.

When we can see these thoughts as well, then we are free of them. We can be free of the doubt thoughts by watching them. We can let go of the "this isn't working" thought when we see it arise in our consciousness, independent of us.

We can become clear, and drop confusion, when we simply watch what is flowing through our awareness.

By watching our thoughts, we can have insights and realizations. To make distance between us and our thoughts is a skill worth cultivating. It can liberate us from the control our minds have over us. It can give us freedom.

There is a lot we can do on our own regarding watching our thoughts. However, this is also where expert guidance comes in handy. We have blind spots and those who have liberated their own minds can help us.

Watching thoughts and seeing them as something temporarily flowing through our awareness is the key to whether we are suffering or living in joy. Believing thoughts can lead to suffering. Being free of them and their influence can allow us to live in joy.

There is a huge difference in our health as well. To feel free in our mind allows the body functions to work more freely. Being free in our emotions allows us to flow with life.

Flow in life supports health. It frees us to do practices that support our health. When the mind is free, the body has the freedom to function without that habitual limitation.

Without limitation, we are free to see what is here for us. We can keep it present. Keep it real. Seeing what is surrounding us, the natural feeling is appreciation for what we have in our lives right now.

3.15

Resting in upward-spiraling currents

Appreciation is simply the choice to see the good in something. Anything has a beneficial aspect, if you only look with innocence.

Find the thing most obvious to you that you can appreciate. You don't have to take on the weighty matters of the world. Appreciate the little things; then you will start to see what to appreciate in bigger things. Make that your mindset.

Appreciate, appreciate, appreciate. Appreciation is an upward-spiraling current.

While resting in this eternal moment and noticing what is here for me, I feel appreciation naturally welling up, all by itself.

Appreciation is a natural result of giving attention to all that is filling our lives, fulfilling us. I see all that is here in my life, and I am filled with wonder and awe. I notice that everything is here to serve me. The appreciation swells to an even greater crescendo.

The things that look like irritations and setbacks are somehow here to serve me. The gifts of opportunities and people stepping in to help me are here to serve me as well. I cannot even fathom the richness of what is serving me now.

The things that look to my little mind as if they are not going my way are certainly here to serve me. They are here not to teach me a lesson, but to allow me to know there is a big picture — and I don't have to know how everything fits in. I can simply love and accept and appreciate that all is working for me to know who I am. To help me rest in this present moment, now and for eternity.

As a bonus, appreciation expands the existing manifestation. That is quite an eye-opener.

By appreciating what is, "what is" has the opportunity to expand to be more of itself. "What is" then creates even more of itself right here, right now. Appreciation brings us into the present to know that all is bountiful and abundant.

The ultimate is to appreciate every moment, for what is here is a perfect serving of what we can enjoy.

Appreciation can also be a part of our daily routine. We can set aside time for appreciation every day, perhaps at the beginning or at the end of the day. Making time for it offers a great reward.

The reward of appreciation is the expansion of the abundance of life into even more abundance. In addition, every moment we appreciate what is here, we are enjoying what is here in the flow of life. We are living in joy. What could be more rewarding than that?

The best way to appreciate every moment is to rest here, in this moment, only here, only now.

What comes out of it may be an appreciation of those loved ones surrounding us. It may turn into calling the loved one, or sending a special note or gift. It may look many ways, depending on the inspiration of the moment.

Once appreciation arises, it flows out and lands somewhere. What naturally flows may be an appreciation for the situations and circumstances of our lives. What flows may be an appreciation for the people in our lives. What naturally flows may be seeing the beauty in this moment, and in creation at this moment.

This not only puts us into a state of awe, it moves us to rest more in this present moment to allow it to have the fullest expression in us and through us.

Appreciation is never just a one-way street.

By expanding joy in the flow of life, appreciation elicits a response from all that is appreciated. Appreciating anything further expands joy, opportunities and awe. The response is gratitude.

Gratitude is the natural response of being appreciated. This is the natural flow. We may have old programs that make glitches in responding with gratitude, but that impulse for gratitude arises naturally from appreciation.

We may want to deny that thing for which we are appreciated. We may be uncomfortable accepting appreciation. We may deflect the appreciation or minimize it. These are all old programs operating. These old programs keep us from experiencing the wonderful experience of being in the flow of life.

When we are resting in this eternal moment, the natural flow is to give thanks for appreciation coming our way. You know that from your experience. You have had that gratitude well up inside when someone gives you praise and appreciation.

When you have been appreciated, and given gratitude to the one who appreciates you, what happens next in this flow? You can probably feel it right now.

Love grows between the appreciator and the one appreciated.

As the one appreciated gives gratitude, the experience further grows in an upward spiral. The gratitude starts as appreciation for the one giving the appreciation, and grows to the outward flow of thanks.

When both parties appreciate each other so much, and have so much gratitude for each other, then is precisely when love blossoms.

This is not romantic love. It is love which is the appreciation for and acceptance of each other exactly as we are. With this appreciation and acceptance, the ability to see more and more unique qualities grows with even more appreciation and acceptance. When it reaches total appreciation and acceptance, it is called unconditional love.

Love is the underlying quality of Nature. Love is underlying our own nature.

This is one thing we can discover, beginning with appreciating what is here and now. As we appreciate, we flow in an upward-spiraling current. Appreciation evolves to gratitude when it is given. Giving and receiving gratitude further spirals upward in a strong current. The next turn of the upward spiral is love.

When we rest in this eternal moment, our appreciation, thanks and love expand. They rise in upward-spiraling currents. Take a turn at it. Again, appreciate what is in your life right now. Just now.

And also, give others the opportunity to give you appreciation, even if you feel that you are already on top of the world. Give them that opportunity to give — and they will feel on top of the world too.

Once we have done that, we see the two faces of giving and receiving. It is not about how much we have or don't have. It is about being open to giving and receiving at the same time, not shutting one off in favor of the other. This is how the upward spiral builds on itself.

In these upward-spiraling currents, don't let the mind get involved. Thoughts from the mind will stop this stream dead in its tracks. Let appreciation take you out of your mind.

Yes, I am telling you to be out of your mind. It is not craziness, it is not irresponsible, it is not being a zombie. When the mind can be the servant while we rest in upward-spiraling currents, we live in joy.

Resting here, right now, in this eternal moment, will take us out of our thoughts. Or perhaps the thoughts can be watched from this useful perspective. That is where I experience the most peace, the most joy.

Living resting in this eternal moment is joy from the cellular level. Each cell is in joy. Then I experience the upwelling of joy in my whole system. Joy permeates all as the currents spiral upwards. Joy is all there is.

Once I started living in joy, I never wanted to live in any other way. Living this way reinforces itself. Living this way is joyful and joy is contagious.

I hope by this time the joy has spread to you. I hope you have caught it, and you are resting in these upward-spiraling currents.

> *"Some say that my teaching is nonsense.*
> *Others call it lofty but impractical.*
> *But to those who have looked inside themselves,*
> *this nonsense makes perfect sense.*
> *And to those who put it into practice,*
> *this loftiness has roots that go deep."*

> — Lao Tzu, *Tao Te Ching*

Afterword

Although resting in this present moment is our natural state, we are accustomed to doing everything but that, and hardly know what that state actually is. For years I would read books — the last one being Eckhart Tolle's *The Power of Now* — and I was inspired to live in the Now. That inspiration always faded, because I was approaching it from my mind, and I did not have a clear experience of what Now is.

That finally changed when I learned what are called Ascension Attitudes. Using these attitudes — which are like a PIN to access the infinite bank account of Now — finally brought me to the clear experience of what I had read about my whole life. My life did begin to flow after I began using these attitudes, both in closed-eye sessions like meditation, as well as with my eyes open. These are the tools that I mentioned in this book.

Using these tools — the attitudes — was not enough. I realized I needed guidance from real people who have gone before me on this path of consciousness. It blew my

249

250 | Antidote to Overwhelm

mind to find a group that was living what other books and teachers were only talking about; they are actually living by totally resting in this present moment! I consider this a very rare thing, and I have immense gratitude that they came into my life.

I am now committed to living my life in this way. In addition, I teach these tools, called Ascension Attitudes, to anyone who knows there is more to life, and is ready to experience it.

This book is an invitation to live your life this way. Rest in this present moment with me. See what becomes of your life and the world.

Resources

If you are ready to experience more out of life, start here:

Dr. Cheryl's
BOOKS
naturopathic physician

AntidoteToOverwhelm.com

Made in the USA
Columbia, SC
14 June 2018